PRAISE FOR
Power: A User's Guide...

"*Power: A User's Guide* is enormously helpful both to those in
positions of power and those who wish to be. Full of enlightening
examples, Julie Diamond's book will inform you and inspire
you to demonstrate your strengths in a positive, authentic way.
I highly recommend it!"

—MARSHALL GOLDSMITH, A *Thinkers 50* Top Ten Global Business Thinker
and New York Times #1 bestselling author of *Triggers*,
MOJO and *What Got You Here Won't Get You There*

"This is a manual for anyone and everyone, not just those in
leadership positions, where the mindful exercise of power is a
daily challenge. Peppered with captivating stories, quotes, and case
studies, *Power: A User's Guide* breaks down the puzzle of power
into bite-sized chunks, and provides guidelines for how to build
and share your power muscles. As a leader of an environmental
organization, where campaigning for positive change is most often
about empowering others or seizing opportunities to shift power
dynamics, this is a book that all activists should read."

—BUNNY MCDIARMID, Executive Director of Greenpeace NZ/Aotearoa

"*Power: A User's Guide* is a tremendously practical guide
on how to navigate organizational life via deeper self-awareness
and active management of ourselves and those around us.
Get ready to get better."

—SYDNEY FINKELSTEIN, Professor of strategy and leadership at the Tuck School
of Business at Dartmouth College and author of
Superbosses: How Exceptional Leaders Master the Flow of Talent

"I urge anyone in a formal leadership role, as well as everyone who wants to live a truly full and meaningful life, to learn and apply Julie Diamond's insights. Full of examples from a broad array of contexts, as well as truly clear, wise and practical advice, this book is rich, accessible, and based on sound psychological knowledge. Reading *Power: A User's Guide* is like engaging in multiple coaching sessions with a wise and trusted therapist—for the price of a book and your time. It is a deal well worth the cost."

—PAT MCLAGAN, Author of *The Shadow Side of Power: Lessons for Leaders* and *Change Is Everybody's Business*

"Elegantly written in a comfortable, narrative style with examples and case studies on every page, Julie Diamond's *Power: A User's Guide* is a practical guide on how to be your best self in your own power. Diamond's years of training and international experience come shining through to offer the best, most prescient and insightful analysis of power I know. As a practical user's guide to power, it doesn't get better."

—JAMES ORBINSKI, MD, Former International President of Medecins Sans Frontieres / Doctors Without Borders, Research Chair in Global Health, and Professor at Laurier University and University of Toronto

"*Power: A User's Guide* is engaging and pulls the reader in to the world of power. I had multiple 'aha!' moments, and by chapter two, I found myself discussing the notions of power and recommending the book to others. Diamond challenged me to become more intentional about my use of power and increased my ability to lead. Anyone searching for substantive leadership guidance that steers clear of fluffiness and hones in on wisdom needs to read this book."

—SARA WESTBROOK, Commander, Portland Police Bureau

"I read *Power: A User's Guide* as my party was struggling against the austerity of Greece's Third Memorandum. During those challenging times, the book provided the tools and perspective I needed to ground my political experience and understand the historical patterns at play. I walked away inspired with a greater awareness of power, unaccompanied by the guilt or fear of abusing it, and seeing its potential to help people communicate and collaborate on creative approaches to our national concerns."

—VASSILIKI KATRIVANOU, SYRIZA Member of Parliament and Chair, Committee on Human Rights

"If you had asked me prior to reading *Power: A User's Guide* whether power (as opposed to leadership) was learnable, I would have said 'no.' I would have been wrong. Deftly mixing psychological concepts, personal and third-party stories, and even pop-culture references (Gollum!), Julie Diamond has produced a book that should be read by anybody and everybody that wants to improve the way they relate to others and the world at large. And, by providing a way to assess your own power—who knew there were so many different types?—and even prescribing a power workout through "doable practices," this is a book I will go back to again and again. I am most excited by what I did not expect: yes, this book provides great value to me professionally, but its greatest value will likely be personally, as I become a better wife, mother, and daughter."

—CALLIE PAPPAS, Vice President & Chief Risk Officer, Schnitzer Steel Industries, Inc.

POWER
A User's Guide

Julie Diamond, Ph.D.

BELLY ● SONG
press
Santa Fe, New Mexico

Published by: Belly Song Press
518 Old Santa Fe Trail, Suite 1 #626, Santa Fe, NM 87505
www.bellysongpress.com

Managing Editor: Lisa Blair
Editor: Matt Lurie
Book cover design: Ann Lowe
Interior design and production: David Moratto

Copyright © 2016 by Julie Diamond

Power: A User's Guide is factually accurate, except that names, locales, and minor aspects of some chapters have been altered to preserve coherence while protecting privacy.

Printed in the United States of America on recycled paper.

First printing 2016. Second printing 2017.

Publisher's Cataloging-in-Publication Data

Diamond, Julie.
Power: a user's guide / Julie Diamond. -- Santa Fe, New Mexico : Belly Song Press, [2016]
    pages ; cm.
    ISBN: 978-0-9966603-0-3 (pbk.) ; 978-0-9966603-1-0 (PDF) ; 978-0-9966603-2-7 (Kindle/Mobipocket) ; 978-0-9966603-3-4 (Epub)
Includes bibliographical references and index.
    Summary: Using power well is more than a matter of good intentions. The path toward ethical, authentic, and effective use of power starts with this book. Combining cutting-edge psychological theory with practical exercises, real-world accounts of leadership challenges, and the author's personal stories from her career as a facilitator and coach, it aims to develop the reader's external authority to navigate high-power roles and responsibilities, and to find personal power within.--Publisher.

    1. Leadership. 2. Power (Social sciences) 3. Executive power. 4. Transformational leadership. 5. Authority. 6. Life skills. 7. Organizational behavior. 8. Management--Psychological aspects. 9. Political corruption. l. Title.

            HM1261 .D53 2016   2015951173
            303.3/4--DC23   1603

                    1 3 5 7 9 10 8 6 4 2

In Loving Memory
Richard M. Diamond

Contents

Section I:
The Principles and Perils of Power

Section II
Getting Started: Find Your Powerprint

Section III
The Guidelines for Power

Acknowledgments

Ideas may start life in an individual head, but like humans, they need social interaction to grow up. They crave contact with others; they need to be befriended and doubted, disagreed with and challenged by other ideas. So while I have been interested in power since my earliest graduate school days, these ideas have grown into adulthood thanks to the socialization efforts of colleagues, friends, teachers, and students.

First and foremost, I would like to thank Professor Richard J. Watts, who in the mid-1980s at the University of Zurich encouraged me to study power. Towards the end of 1985, as I was finishing my *Lizentiat*, he suggested I focus my doctorate on the study of power in discourse. And so I did, investigating what I called *rank* at the time in small group interaction.

I was fortunate to be in Zurich during the evolution of Process-oriented Psychology, an enormously effective and creative method for individual and group development. It was without a doubt one of my greatest fortunes (if not *the* greatest fortune) to be able to be part of the earliest group of students of Arnold ("Arny") Mindell—physicist, Jungian analyst, and author—who devoted his career to developing Process-oriented Psychology, or Process Work as it is familiarly called.

Arny incorporated the concepts of rank and power into his group process methods, and created a psychological framework for understanding how rank dynamics played out in the context of group conflict and organizational life. He elucidated the different sources of personal power: psychological and spiritual rank. His work on the "psychology of rank" and how it manifests in conflict, interaction, and relationship is foundational to this book. I am deeply indebted not only to his ideas and his body of work, but also to his teaching and friendship over the years. He used his power as a teacher, supervisor, and therapist to encourage and inspire his students to be creative, bold, and adventurous in the pursuit of their passions.

I owe a great deal to my friend and co-developer of the Power[2] Leaderlab, Lesli Mones. Lesli and I have spent the last five years unpacking the problems of power, leadership, and learning, to create coaching programs, assessments, and training for executives, banging our heads (our own and occasionally each other's) against the wall trying to figure out ways to make it practical, useable, and relevant for leaders. Many ideas and formulations here have been nurtured, if not directly inspired, by our collaboration. And though it is difficult, with that level of collaboration, to disentangle the threads of our work, I have tried, whenever possible, to give credit for her unique insights and formulations.

I am thankful for the privilege to have taught and developed programs in Process-oriented Psychology. My role as faculty member, supervisor, and developer and director of some of the training programs in Process Work was foundational to my career. I had the privilege of teaching internationally, learning from many gifted practitioners, and developing close friendships with practitioners, students, and teachers in the international community of Process-oriented Psychology.

I owe special thanks to my fellow teachers and students at the Process Work Institute of Portland. It seems much of what I know now about power was either learned, practiced, or deepened while working on the creation of the Institute and its training programs.

My deep appreciation goes to colleagues with whom I spent de-cades working on the development of our training programs: Dawn Menken, Jan Dworkin, Joe Goodbread, Kate Jobe, Herb Long, Amy Mindell, Rhea, Stephen Schuitevoerder, Max Schupbach, and Sonja Straub. I would also like to thank my colleagues in Zurich, at the original Forschungsgesellschaft fuer Prozessorienterte Psychologie, and my good friends, fellow teachers, and students in the Australia-New Zealand Process Orientated Psychology Association who have generously invited me to teach in their program, giving me an op-portunity to test out many of my ideas.

Over the past ten years, I have had the opportunity to apply my work inside organizations and on projects with others that have been enriching, inspiring, and critical to the development of this work. I thank you for the privilege of working with and learning from you: Liesbeth Gerritsen and Commander Sara Westbrook at the Portland Police Bureau, Ian Curtin at The Inner Activist, Shakil Choudhury and Annahid Dashtgard at Anima Leadership, Stephan Dilchert, Assistant Professor of Management at the Zicklin School of Business, Baruch College, Deniz Ones, Professor & Distinguished McKnight University Professor at the University of Minnesota, Sheelagh Davis formerly at British Columbia Nurses Union, and Liz Skelton and Geoff Aigner at Social Leadership Australia.

To my readers and reviewers, who offered their valuable sugges-tions and insights, I owe a huge thanks. Shakil Choudhury, Annahid Dashtgard, Paul Donovan, Jan Dworkin, Liz Scott, and Cindy Trawin-ski, thank you, each and every one of you, for your generosity. You actually read the manuscript, carefully and thoroughly, and enhanced this book with your critiques, suggestions, comments, and occasional jokes. You pushed and prodded for more examples, diagrams, and explanations. You caught glaring omissions, muddled concepts, tautological tangles, and profoundly perplexing sentences. Above all, you helped me see the book I was trying to write. Thank you for your honesty, clarity, and guidance.

I am fortunate to have friends and colleagues who, at various stages of this work, have shared their ideas and stories, pointed me to research, given me examples, talked over concepts, and helped make this work come to life through their support: Vassiliki Katrivanou, Annahid Dashtgard, Shakil Choudhury, Rho Sandberg, Rick Jaech, Errol Amerasekera, Lukas Hohler, Karen Salter, Jean Luc Moreau, Alan Richardson, Miguel Vasquez, Melissa Martin, Andrea Scharf, Jim Adler, and Kevin Jones. Cindy Trawinski has added enormously to this book by helping me think deeply about its meaning, impact, and how to communicate it to the larger world. I am fortunate for your friendship and wisdom.

And thank you to you readers and commenters on my blog, *A User's Guide to Power*. I did not know how important it would be to me, when I launched the blog in 2008, to have your interest and participation.

My production team deserves much of the credit for helping this book see the light of day. First and foremost, I thank my lucky stars to have found Matt Lurie, gifted writer, editor, content creator, and communication wizard, without whose help I could not have done this. If this book has value, then it's due to Matt's extraordinary ability to cut through the clutter, and bring out the gem of an idea, buried somewhere in a pile of words. Matt also had the psychotherapist's gift of knowing when to provide reassurance, positive feedback, and a dash of humor, when it all got to be too much.

David Bedrick and Lisa Blair at Belly Song Press have been a huge source of guidance and support. Their understanding not only of the publishing process but also of the writer's process makes me want to write a book a year just to be able to work with them on a regular basis. This book has benefitted enormously by their commitment, attention to quality, and technical know-how.

I'd also like to thank Katie Fuller, my administrative assistant and external hard disk who is always one step ahead of me, for her incredible attention to detail and flair for organization. She manages much of the day-to-day business, and I feel very lucky to have had her join my team.

I am grateful to my friends who encouraged me, fed me, dragged me out of the house when I needed it, and helped me remember the most important things in life, in this order: love, nature, and food: John Posey, Dennis Laird, Tom O'Neill, Kathy O'Neill, Dawn Menken, Lesli Mones, Jan Dworkin, Sonja Straub, Cindy Trawinski, Andrea Scharf, and Jim and Ursula Adler.

My mother, Nancy Diamond, supports me in every way possible. Her fierce love and belief in me sustains me, and always has. Though I can't prove it, I'd like to think I got my work ethic and gift of endurance from her. I am sorry my father, Richard Diamond, is not alive to read my words of appreciation for him. He spent his life fighting for justice and trying to make the world a better place, through the power of the written word. His passion for a better world fuels mine.

Finally, nothing is worth doing without the love and friendship of my wife and best friend, Caroline Spark. She encouraged me, discussed concepts with me, consoled me, challenged me when needed, and never (much) complained when writing and work took me away from home. It would have been more than enough to have her love and support in my life, but in addition, she inspires me to reach for the stars, in word and deed, by reaching for hers. *Dayenu.*

Introduction

Power Corrupts — Absolutely, but Not Inevitably

~⌒

Mastering others is strength;
mastering yourself is true power.

—LAO TZU

At 26,000 feet above sea level, your body starts to die. Here, at an altitude known as the "death zone"—only 3,000 feet below the summit of Mount Everest—oxygen levels are a third of what they are at sea level. You have about two days before you run out of air.

As your body starts to deteriorate, your mind abandons you. Hypoxia, low atmospheric pressure, means less oxygen is entering your brain. Your judgment is impaired. You become confused, your balance starts to falter, and you begin to hallucinate. You are losing your mind—right when you need it most.

Just like the oxygen-thin atmosphere on the upper reaches of Mount Everest, the rarified atmosphere of high power and status alters our minds, diminishing our judgment and distorting our perceptions. As we attain power, we develop an illusory sense of control. Our belief in our own ideas increases while our interest in others' feedback and emotions decreases.

But here's the difference: on Everest, climbers at high altitude feel awful. They know they're dying. They suffer pounding headaches. They vomit. They become dizzy and weak, lose coordination, and have trouble standing or walking.

In the embrace of high power, we feel great. The more altered we become, the better we feel. High rank and power lower our inhibitions and prime us to act. Our confidence soars as our perceptions grow more distorted. Our self-esteem rises, while our self-awareness decreases. Our capacity to feel empathy for others lessens, just as the influence we have over them increases. The more we need guidance from others, the less we want it.

Power is fundamental to human existence. History is told as a series of power struggles: wars, coups, upsets, victories, losses, gains, landmark decisions. Writers, philosophers, economists, political scientists, sociologists, and psychologists are obsessed with and fascinated by power. It's a force we've recognized as part of our condition since day one. For as long as people have formed groups, there have been relationships structured by power, hierarchy, dominance, status, and control. For millennia, people have wielded power to found cultures, level empires, and champion social causes.

Power permeates all aspects of our social life, with friends, lovers, family members, and co-workers. Power is fundamental to leadership, parenting, education, the helping professions, law enforcement, and many other vocations. Power is not only a social phenomenon, but also a psychological one. When we struggle with ourselves over competing drives and desires, feelings of inferiority and superiority, and with habits, addictions, and discipline, power is at play.

Power has as many definitions as it does manifestations. In fact, it is one of the most contested concepts in sociology. Max Weber, the German sociologist, defined power as the ability to assert one's will over others, in spite of resistance. This classic "power-over" definition has been challenged and critiqued by later scholars, including sociologists such as Steven Lukes, Peter Bachrach, Morton

Baratz, and Michel Foucault, who have identified more subtle forms of control: the shaping of interests, setting of social agendas, and determining of cultural values. Members of the media, for instance, exercise this subtle form of power by choosing to broadcast certain images and stories, thus promoting certain values. Omission and neglect are also acts of power, as they create the appearance of urgency for some issues and cast others as unimportant or nonexistent. Bachrach and Baratz defined this dimension of power beyond "Person A" asserting their will over "Person B," but as the methods whereby:

> [Person] A devotes his energies to creating or reinforcing social and political values and institutional practices that limit the scope of the political process to public consideration of only those issues which are comparatively innocuous to A.[1]

These definitions are concerned with what power *does*, but another set of definitions concerns the kinds of power people use to control or influence others. John French and Bertram Raven's theory of the five bases or sources of power is one of the most cited descriptions of power.[2] French and Raven identify three kinds of formal power, and two kinds of personal power. Formal power can come through coercive means (threat or force), awards (incentive or reward), or legitimate means (the authority of one's position or role within an organization). Personal power, meanwhile, can be expert (one's knowledge, skills, or expertise), or referent (trust, relationship, and affiliations).

How do I define power? Because this book focuses on how power is used by everyone, and not just those in designated roles, the definition needs to include both formal and informal—or personal—power. So, for our purposes, this basic definition will suffice, at least for now: power is our capacity to impact and influence our environment.

Impact and influence can occur through both active and passive means; to paraphrase Paul Watzlawick, one cannot *not* influence.[3]

Whatever we do impacts others. And we use many kinds of power to do so: power that is bestowed by virtue of our social status or position, and power that is grown and developed: our personal power, the force of our personality, social skills, and emotional intelligence. Roles of authority and external social status or rank bestow power, but power also resides within us, in our ability to persevere under hardship and make decisions that alter the course of our fates as well as the lives around us.

Regardless of how we define it, like fire, power hypnotizes and scares us. At a primal level we understand that, left unchecked, it will consume us. Lord Acton's famous observation, "Power tends to corrupt, and absolute power corrupts absolutely," is backed by more than two decades of research demonstrating what high power does to people. Power has an insidious "shadow side." It carries with it the means for its own abuse.

Social psychologists such as Deborah Gruenfeld at Stanford Graduate School, Adam Galinksy at Northwestern University's Kellogg School of Management, Joe Magee at New York University, Nathanael Fast at University of Southern California, and Susan Fiske at Princeton are beginning to discover how this shadow side of power operates. In their research, they've found that people primed to wield more power display higher levels confidence, are less concerned with others' opinions and feelings, and take their subjective perceptions more seriously than they do others'. They have greater mental freedom and are more ready to act. And, when they do act, they do so with decisiveness and confidence. Psychologist Arnold Mindell, who has applied the psychology of rank and power to large group dynamics and conflict resolution, says it bluntly: Rank is a drug.[4]

Yet these very things that can make power corrosive also make for great leadership. Leaders, innovators, and social activists need confidence, decisiveness, and a strong sense of self-belief to make decisions and drive movements forward. They need to be ready for action, even when they lack all the necessary information to make a careful decision.

But without self-awareness, these behaviors and states of mind dramatically increase the risk of misusing authority.

It's not just leaders who are prone to this error. Power doesn't emerge merely from your position; it emerges from your social status, your standing in your friendship group, and even your personality. Society grants status to you based on your skin color, gender, and social class. Your skill set or seniority in your workplace or community may also endow you with high status, even if you don't occupy a leadership role. Maybe you're the person at work who can fix the Internet network when it goes down; or the calm, wise friend others turn to when they're in trouble. You might have power in your relationship because you're more independent than your partner, or because you're more demanding and expressive.

Power arises from making friends and attracting others. Sometimes, even lingering effects from childhood can give you a sense of power—your status as the oldest sibling, for instance, or doing well in school, or being the one who was good at sports that everyone wanted on their kickball team.

Wherever you get it from, power is hard to get right. Wielding power over someone or something—whether you're running a Fortune 500 company, raising children, or coaching a junior high basketball team—is a tough job. And the more there is at stake, the harder it is to get right. The failure rate of leaders shows just how difficult it is to operate while in power's death zone: half the executives promoted to the highest levels of power fail within two years. Elected leaders don't seem to do too well either; their abuses of power are daily fodder for the media.

These are just the abuses of power that come to light. Others misuse power every day, closer to home, and don't make headlines: bullies at work, school, and in the home; teachers who favor some students over others; colleagues who derail meetings; over-controlling and over-protective parents; partners and spouses who are demanding, or emotionally abusive and emotionally inept; jealous bosses; and others still.

Make no mistake, however: not all of these individuals realize the impact of their power, or that they have power at all. Misusing power is as much an act of omission as it is an act of commission. Many people enter positions of power intent on doing things differently. They insist they won't become corrupted or abuse their authority. They want to be an empowering leader. As parents, they swear against becoming disciplinarians. They try to be relational and egalitarian. So they tread lightly, attempting to minimize the footprint of their authority.

But not using power isn't the same as using it well. Underusing power makes just as big a mess as overusing it. Teachers who don't take control of classroom dynamics let unsafe atmospheres detract from learning. Team leaders who won't make decisions allow projects to degenerate into frustrating and pointless endeavors. Parents who don't set limits inadvertently teach their children they'll always get their way in relationships, and the children never develop the self-discipline and frustration tolerance necessary to work towards goals. A boss who refuses to deal with the conflict on her team, hoping it'll just "work itself out," is at risk of losing valuable team members.

About Me

I have spent my entire professional life studying power. Even as a child, I was drawn to issues of power, motivated by a keen sense of social justice. Growing up in the 1960s, I was aware of poverty and racism, of civil rights struggles and anti-war marches, which unfolded nightly on the news. I watched footage of assassinations, protests, police clubbing protestors in Chicago, of Watts and Detroit erupting in flames. Wherever I looked, I saw what seemed to be the effects of unequal power relations. Too young to march in the anti-war and civil rights protests of the 1960s, I nonetheless declared myself a Marxist in high school, and earned the title "Class Radical" in my 1977 graduating class.

In college, my interest in power and politics took a sharp turn. Campus life at Antioch College in the 1970s would have been a perfect launching pad for political activism, but instead, I became disillusioned by student activism. Though my fellow activists and I could point to institutional and state abuse, it seemed to stop short of our own behavior. We were exempt from examining our own methods. Our ego struggles and poor use of power were excusable. As long as we were fighting the good fight, it didn't matter whether our methods were good as well.

This troubled me. I thought that our own use of power should be a topic of consideration. But I was accused of sidestepping bigger issues, of neglecting the priorities, and fundamentally, being a lousy activist—which I suppose I was.

The conflict ultimately drove me inwards, from politics to the study of the mind. Inspired by my friends and their interests in the unconscious, I found a home in psychology, looking into the dreams, emotions, and motivations that drove people. I wondered if the solution to the problems of injustice could be found within. Could social change start with individual awareness?

This question led me to Zurich, Switzerland, in 1981, to study psychology with Arnold Mindell, Jungian analyst and teacher. At the time, Mindell was expanding the boundaries of analytic psychology to encompass all dimensions of an individual's life: not only the inner world of thoughts and feelings, but also relationships, social relations, group dynamics, movement, and bodily experiences.

Simultaneous to my psychology studies with Mindell, I started graduate school at the University of Zurich, and it was there that I decided to formally study power. With the support of my professor, Richard Watts, I focused my sociolinguistic research on power in social discourse. I was fascinated by how people negotiated power in interaction, often in semi-conscious or unconscious ways. Contrary to the popular ways of discussing power as related to position, authority, seniority, and other forms of status, I saw that in interaction, it was fluid and negotiable—up for grabs, moment by moment. For this reason, I used the word *rank* in my research, as I investigated the linguistic strategies people used to negotiate their rank.

After exploring the topic in my dissertation, I decided I wanted to be a practitioner rather than an academic. I spent the next two decades working with individuals and groups in various roles, as a facilitator, psychotherapist, supervisor, coach, and trainer. Though I wasn't studying power directly, my work gave me more insight into people's behavior, and shed light on what flummoxed me in college: the disconnect between what we say we believe, and what we actually do.

But it was when I stepped into a leadership role myself, as the Director of Training at the Process Work Institute of Portland, that I stumbled upon a missing piece in my study of power: the experience from the perspective of a leader. Though my role was miniscule compared to many leaders, I felt what it was like to have the weight of responsibility for others and for an organization on my shoulders. No amount of study or working with others could have helped me understand this inner experience of power, of being in the crosshairs of public opinion, under pressure for your performance, and subject to the projections of others. I gained greater empathy for the role of power holder, and saw and felt how much the role itself affects the person within it.

I had come full circle. My interests in psychology, power, and social change collided together in the field of leadership. I shifted my practice, and began to focus more or less exclusively on leadership.

Over the past twenty years, I have coached, consulted, and trained CEOs, police officers, military leaders, politicians, union leaders, nonprofit leaders, supervisors, managers, educators, therapists, religious leaders, social activists, and parents—just about every possible leadership role. I see now that it's possible to use power effectively and responsibly. Anyone can be a fair and mindful leader, parent, or teacher. The reverse is true as well: anyone can get caught in one of power's numerous snares. It all depends on the user, on their motives, awareness, and ability to understand and work with their emotions.

Using power well depends on becoming aware of our behavior, and of those often-unconscious feelings that drive it: beliefs, fears, and attitudes. As this book will demonstrate, using power well starts with self-awareness.

Self-awareness is key because power's insidious shadow side is covert and subtle. It's extremely easy for us all to fall into any one of them. In my twenty-five years of consulting, training, and coaching, I've seen several common power traps that people tend to fall into:

- ***Using power before earning it.*** When you think authority alone makes you the leader, you lose legitimacy. Whether concerned to make your mark, driven by ego, pressured to get something done, or just anxious to be accepted, you embark on a new initiative before gaining the trust of your followers. Yet you haven't taken the time to get people on board; you haven't cultivated relationships, communicated your ideas, nor have you asked for input or feedback. You believe people will follow you by dint of your role, but you haven't earned their trust, and this diminishes your authority.

- ***Sidestepping authority.*** Determined not to misuse power, you avoid taking a stand. You don't make the tough call. You debate ideas endlessly, afraid to decide on one. You avoid difficult conversations. You try to support and collaborate with subordinates, but fail to hold people accountable or help them grow. You don't want to limit others' creativity, or be oppressive. So instead, you just create confusion. You undermine team morale when you don't set limits, when you let discussions meander, and when you allow people to derail the agenda. When decisions keep changing, no one on your team knows what's expected of them. It's stressful and chaotic working with and for someone who doesn't embrace their power.

- ***Using too much ammo.*** You identify as the weaker party. You start every encounter from a one-down position, convinced you won't be able to get your point across. So your first salvo is already an escalated one: an accusation, defense, or attack. You're certain the other is criticizing or challenging you. You therefore fail to realize that you are actually the aggressor. It becomes a vicious cycle: you interpret the other's defensive response as an act of power, and escalate the conflict. In your mind, because you have less power, you fail to see how antagonistic you are, and set off runaway conflicts wherever you go.

- ***Using power to boost your low self-worth.*** You use your rank like a drug: it makes you feel good to have people listen to and look up to you. People's admiration and eagerness to talk to you makes you feel important. Any doubt you have about your intelligence is momentarily alleviated when people pay attention to your ideas. If you have trouble making friends and fear rejection, then the interest of your students, clients, or patients can be a handy shortcut to relationships. If you feel weak, your righteous activism and justifiable anger lends you an instant hit of strength. Over time, though, you lose the muscle to do the work necessary for your own emotional development, and become reliant on your role and the judgment of those around you.

- ***Buying your own pitch.*** As the leader, you can create a culture where your ideas aren't challenged. You can cherry-pick the feedback that confirms what you already think. You measure progress with your own yardstick and treat your problems with your own medicine, but don't trust others' advice or methods to evaluate how things are going. You have fallen victim to self-confirming beliefs, and your high-ranking role keeps you shielded from social contexts outside your influence, limiting the opportunity to engage with challenging opinions or ideas. Like a rock star surrounded by an entourage, over time you lose touch with reality. In return, your organization becomes cultish, insular, and out of touch.

- **Satisfying your self-interest.** A high-ranking role makes it easy to satisfy personal needs. If you're a professor, you can compel your graduate students to take over undesirable tasks; if you're a boss, subordinates can run errands for you. As a leader, you can use your power to set a schedule or assign projects in ways that favor you or your friends. You may not follow all the rules, but you expect others to. You promote friends, relatives, or favorites into key positions. You think that asking for a few favors is harmless, but you don't realize (or don't want to realize) that subordinates aren't free to refuse your requests. Ultimately, your inability to separate personal from organizational interests undermines your performance, as well as the respect others have for you.

- **Simply overdoing it.** Like Narcissus, it's easy to become mesmerized by our reflections when we occupy high-ranking roles. The lecturing professor falls in love with the sound of her own voice and fails to see she's lost the interest of the class. The boss micromanages and refuses to delegate, believing himself smarter than everyone else. The mother becomes controlling and overprotective, unable to trust her children to think for themselves. The social activist becomes righteous and unable to collaborate with allies, convinced his position is the only correct position. The expert starts to believe her genius applies across all disciplines, handing out advice about everything—even topics beyond her scope of knowledge.

- **Not holding yourself accountable.** Because no one holds you accountable, you may not either. You don't curb your bad behavior. You let your temper out, yell, and act rude under stress. You don't admit your mistakes but blame others, or the environment, when things go wrong. You spread rumors and take credit for others' work—or your subordinates', threatened by their accomplishment. You seek revenge on those who disagree with you. You treat people poorly, criticize or shame others in public, and basically fail to manage your emotions under stress.

The Taboo Against Power

If power is so difficult to wield, why don't we learn more about it in school? Why haven't we been taught to cultivate and use power responsibly? We get promoted, earn seniority, get elected to public office, and become doctors or teachers—all without guidance or training in the use of power.

Leadership training is a multibillion-dollar industry, with hundreds of world-class executive development programs and countless courses, books, blogs, and tools. And yet, scant attention is paid to the psychological impact of power. Even parents enter the biggest leadership role of their lives—perhaps the biggest there is—responsible for the well-being and character of their children, with little or no training in the parental use of power. Given power's enormous cost when it is misused in our organizations, and in our larger world, it's puzzling there's no "Driver's Ed" for power users, especially for those we entrust with our lives and welfare: teachers, health care providers, police, parents, politicians, and public servants.

Why? Why do we ignore the topic of using power?

I see two reasons:

1) **Power has a bad rap.** Power has been the chief troublemaker throughout human history. Though the days of monarchs are waning, our world still suffers from the devastation of current or past despotic leadership, corporate fraud, government malfeasance, and the bullying behavior of those we deal with on a daily basis: managers, teachers, parents, and peers. Because of the immense damage done in its name, we blame power and do our best to avoid it. In most organizations I work with, people tiptoe around the word itself, and prefer euphemisms such as *influence, authority, leverage*, or *strength*.

2) **We consider abuse of power a dispositional malady.** We are primed to look for the source of badness in the personality, to pathologize bad behavior. We call those who abuse power "psychopaths" and "narcissists." We analyze the perpetrator's personality and childhood, looking for the cause of the disease: Does she have a personality disorder? Is he an ego-maniac? Was she bullied as a child? Giving it a diagnosis or finding an etiology provides false comfort that *we* won't catch the disease. *We* don't have that condition. It makes us feel safer about our own use of power, confident we'd never embezzle funds, harass subordinates, or use campaign con-tributions to cover up an extramarital affair. But people who misuse power are not sadists, lunatics, or psychopaths. People who misuse power are ordinary people like you and me.

Power, like sex and death, is a taboo topic. As with all taboos, we have developed an irrational relationship with power. We hate it yet crave it. We criticize those in power while striving to get more for ourselves. We eye anyone in authority with suspicion, but fail to reflect on our own uses of power. We overestimate others' influence and underestimate our own. We do away with hierarchy and replace it with flat teams or consensus but then tolerate the endlessly cycling debates, cliques, preferentialism, and political maneuvering that result when power goes underground.

No matter how much we hate it, no matter how much evil has been done in its name, we cannot do away with power. We cannot pretend it doesn't exist by flattening teams, abolishing hierarchies, or acting collegial with our subordinates.

Power is not a social artifact. It belongs to the human condition, no more uncommon or complex than jealousy, love, or attraction. We can ban office romances, but love still flourishes. Similarly, we can do away with hierarchies, or enforce codes of conduct, but power struggles still flourish. Power is an interpersonal and psychological dynamic that forces its way into every interaction, from the boardroom to the bedroom.

Power is neither good nor bad; it is energy, a human drive to shape the world, influence others, and make an impact. We *need* power. Power may be difficult to master, but it's vital to have. It's generative and creative. When people have more power at work, they become more engaged, imaginative, and inspired. When citizens are empowered, they become mobilized and can make sweeping social changes, even ousting despotic leaders. Power makes parents effective, teachers amazing, and students successful. It helps us collaborate with opponents to work across chasms of difference and create solutions for our most complex problems. Power means raising social awareness, standing up to bullies, advocating for the oppressed, fighting for and protecting civil and human rights. It is the key to equitable workplaces, successful teams, and innovative environments.

We need power for our personal growth. We need to feel powerful enough on the inside to make friends, get along with difficult people, solve conflicts, and repair hurt relationships. It is our inner sense of power that we turn to when facing tragedy. We might get a job because of credentials or family name, but we keep the job and succeed in it due to our inner power.

Power is the force we have to participate fully, creatively, and passionately in our own lives. It allows us find the learning in set-backs, hope after defeat, and balance after life delivers a challenging blow. We use power every day to make choices, from the mundane —"eggs or oatmeal?"—to the life-altering decisions concerning jobs, partners, and long-term objectives. Indeed, we use power to motivate ourselves, set goals, and push ourselves towards those goals. Power, used well, can be an act of self-love, and owning your authority and influence is the necessary precondition to self-development.

Who Should Read This Book

Ed Viesturs is one of the top high-altitude mountaineers in the world. He has successfully reached the summits of each of the world's fourteen 8000-meter (26,247 feet, or just under 5 miles above sea level) peaks without supplemental oxygen twenty-one times, including Mount Everest—seven times.

Viesturs doesn't call climbing Everest "summiting," as many climbers do. He calls it "a round trip." His motto: "Getting to the top is optional. Getting down is mandatory."

Viesturs remains humble in the face of the mountain's extreme conditions. Even meters from the summit, he's never shied away from turning back if conditions are too severe. As much as he would probably like to stand at the top of the world after years of grueling physical preparation and huge financial investment, he won't sum-mit unless conditions are right. He knows it's not about him. There are others to think about. He won't put his team in jeopardy, nor will he put his ambition before the well-being of his family.

Viesturs has not only mastered the death zone of Everest, but also the death zone of power. He knows how to stay aware, to keep his priorities straight and his ego in check. He doesn't let fame, fortune, or success tempt him otherwise. He doesn't let the goal obscure his values, even when victory seems within reach.

This book is for anyone who, like Viesturs, desires to conquer their own death zone. It establishes guidelines for enacting authority with dignity, using power responsibly and with awareness, and unleashing the creative potential and generative capacity that power gives us.

You have this book in your hands because you wrestle with the problems of leadership and power—whether you work in business, education, the nonprofit world, law enforcement, a religious institution, or government, or simply want to make a happier home life for yourself and your family. You aspire to be better at what you do, achieve more and have a greater impact, but need to know how to navigate the death zone of power first.

You may be a...

- **Social entrepreneur or innovator.** Your goal is to effect large-scale social change. You see what's not working and want to open up new avenues and opportunities. But to do so, you need to collaborate with others, enlist allies, convert skeptics, and engage with stakeholders, many of whom follow different—sometimes opposing—agendas.

- **Transformational leader.** Your leadership philosophy is about empowering your employees, increasing engagement, and creating a meaningful workplace by enhancing others' self-efficacy and creativity.

- **Manager, boss, or supervisor.** You need power to influence, impress, and motivate others below and above you. You have a vision, but need "buy-in." You seek to engage your team, get the support of the higher-ups, gain traction for your ideas, and be taken seriously.

- ***Coach, consultant, or advisor working with leaders.*** Your role is to help those in power stay on course, and so you need power yourself to be impactful, hold difficult conversations, and give feedback—all without colluding with or becoming enmeshed with those whom you're meant to advise.

- ***Doctor, educator, lawyer, parent, trainer, or therapist.*** Your expertise and wisdom earn you the regard of your students, customers, clients, patients, or children. To avoid falling prey to their admiration and awe, you need to develop awareness of your own limitations and ego needs, and to learn strategies for using your wisdom and power in the service of others.

- ***Political activist, politician, or community organizer.*** You want to change the way things are in your community, school, neighborhood, city, or country. You need power to fight on behalf of others and against the status quo, without becoming tyrannical, righteous, or superior in your own authority.

- ***Clergy or religious leader.*** You have placed yourself at the service of your community. You need to be able to use the authority vested in you to counsel, console, guide, and direct others in their spiritual lives, without allowing yourself to over-identify with the spiritual power you channel.

- ***Military or law enforcement officer.*** Your job is to protect and defend. You take enormous risks and place yourself in jeopardy on behalf of strangers. You also have the authority to use force—deadly force—and with this authority comes profound responsibility. You need power to stay aware and mindful under stress and danger, to manage your emotions, and to hold yourself accountable to the public that places their trust in you.

Whatever you do, whoever you are, you have this book in your hands because you recognize that using power effectively and positively is a core competency in life. You want to grow your power and become effective in its use. This book will teach you how to develop your power, infuse your position of authority with sustainable and effective power, and avoid power's dangerous and ever-present traps.

A Note on Terms

In this book, I frequently use the terms "rank," "authority," and "power." In one sense, they are synonyms and, in some cases, I use the words "rank" and "power" interchangeably. But there are some important differences to spell out.

As I described above, in my doctoral research I chose the word *rank* because it expresses relativity. I use the word in this book as well, when discussing power relative to others, as in a ranking system. Rank suggests not a static idea of power, but a dynamic network of power in motion, shifting up and down a hierarchy. And hierarchy depends on the given context: there are hierarchies in a workplace, but also in friendship groups, societies, and families. Rank is also sometimes used to refer to the total of all our different kinds of power (social status, positional, personal) because these kinds of power are relative and dynamic as well.

Authority refers to the power that we have that rests on some sort of legitimacy, whether explicit in the role we occupy, or implicit in the sense that people agree to follow us. Your position at work gives you authority, as does your role as parent. But while authority is granted, it is not automatic. People can behave poorly in their roles, and thus lose their legitimacy.

Finally, I use the word *power* in its philosophical sense: as force, impact, and influence. I also use it specifically to describe the different categories of impact and influence: social status, positional power, personal power, and so forth.

How to Use the *User's Guide*

This book is called a "User's Guide" because it's designed like a technical manual on power. You can go directly to any section for specific instructions, or you can read the guide conventionally from start to finish.

Here's what you can expect to gain from each section and chapter:

Section I, "The Principles and Perils of Power," provides a broad overview of power: what it is, where it comes from, and how it operates. This is the theoretical section, written for those who are interested in the mechanics of power and the theory underlying its principles.

Chapter 1, "Under the Influence: What Makes Power Corrupt?" shows why and how power corrupts us. It outlines the emotional impact and psychological influences of power that lead us astray, no matter how good our intentions may be.

Chapter 2, "Motive: What Makes People Corruptible?" explores how and why we fall prey to power's corrupting pull. It shows the differences between "positional" or "social power" and "personal power," and explains how power use is driven by our feelings: The more powerful we *feel*, the better we use our power; conversely, the less powerful we feel, the greater the chance we'll misuse power.

Section II, "Getting Started: Finding Your Powerprint," is a hands-on exercise for discovering your power arsenal.

Chapter 3, "Powerprints: Your Unique Picture of Power," describes the complex system of power. Using case studies, it presents the concept of *Powerprint*: your unique map of the different kinds of power you have, where they come from, and the influences from childhood that continue to impact your use of power today.

Chapter 4, "Find Your Powerprint," sets up a self-reflection activity designed to help you create your own Powerprint. Here, you can decide whether to flip to the **Appendix** or continue forward without your Powerprint. The activity will help you identify all the kinds of powers you have, your special strengths and liabilities. It will allow you to understand which of the rules of power are most useful to you in Chapters 4–8, which focus on developing your use of power.

Section III, "The Guidelines for Power," presents the specific guidelines for developing, using, and sharing your power. In each chapter of the section, you will also find "Doable Practices," which are exactly what they sound like: practical ways you can train yourself on and experiment with the guidelines in your day-to-day life.

Chapter 5, "First, Cultivate Your Traits," lays out the steps for developing your personal power. Without a solid foundation in personal power, you are at the mercy of others' judgments, popular sentiment, and social norms—all of which fluctuate from moment to moment, and all of which lie outside your control. The rules of power in Chapter 5 will help you sow and cultivate your personal power, an inner sense of authority that remains stable and durable regardless of your outer situation.

Chapter 6, "Use Your Personal Power," presents the next set of power laws: gaining legitimacy and the respect of others. While personal power doesn't depend on others for its value, you can undermine it by misusing your positional power. It is easy to fall under the spell of positional and social power, using the perks of privilege as a shortcut for personal gain. This section presents the steps to wielding your power legitimately to avoid squandering your legitimacy and, ultimately, your personal power.

Chapter 7, "Share Your Personal Power," concentrates on the ways you can turn your organization, community, or family into a place of "positive power." Power provides us with opportunities: access to money, people, information, and resources. Along with these perks, we have greater freedom to act, but often with less supervision or oversight. This deadly cocktail of opportunity and immunity creates a constant conflict of interest. To reduce the chance for misuse or abuse to occur, we need to take active measures, by creating structures and procedures that mitigate the conflicts of interest. This last set of power laws offers five critical steps for limiting opportunity and making our organizations places of positive and healthy authority.

Like all technical manuals, *A User's Guide* ends with a section on "Troubleshooting." Some uses of power present exceptional circumstance, and **Chapter 8, "Troubleshooting: Special Power Challenges,"** addresses three specific challenges associated with power. Being among the first representative of your demographic group to occupy a position of power can be a lonely and difficult road. If you're the first of your gender, race, ethnicity, sexual orientation, or other social status to occupy a high-power position, you are subject to stereotypes, unrealistic expectations, and criticism. The second challenge deals another great test of power—using power with bosses, peers, colleagues, and other stakeholders over whom you have no authority. The last challenge is for those in a helping or consulting profession. When power flows from your expertise and you occupy a role that involves a degree of intimacy and dependency, you need to be awake to its potential pitfalls. It's very easy to take advantage of someone's dependency on our wisdom when we take on such roles as therapist, financial advisor, lawyer, coach, consultant, or doctor.

Chapter 9, "Power Checklist," is a summary of the book and a practical checklist for power users. After reviewing the basics and assembling the rules of power with your own Powerprint, you will be ready to head out, use your superpowers, and create the world you want to create.

THE PRINCIPLES AND PERILS OF POWER

*There is no meaning to life except the meaning man
gives his life by the unfolding of his powers.*
—ERICH FROMM

1

Under the Influence:
What Makes Power Corrupt?

Nearly all men can stand adversity,
but if you want to test a man's character, give him power.
—ABRAHAM LINCOLN

Rank is a drug.
—ARNOLD MINDELL

In the summer of 1971, Philip Zimbardo, a young psychology professor at Stanford University, wanted to test the classic "nature–nurture" question of power: do people abuse their power because of their personality or because of the situation?

Armed with funding from the U.S. Office of Naval Research, Zimbardo recruited a sample of college students and randomly assigned each the role of prisoner or prison guard. Because he wanted to make his experiment as authentic as possible, he constructed an elaborate role-play, complete with outfits for participants and a makeshift prison in the basement of the psychology building on campus. He even recruited the Palo Alto Police Department. Officers "arrested" each "prisoner" in their homes, took the prisoners down to the precinct, charged them with armed robbery, and went through the full booking procedure: mug shots, fingerprints, strip searches. Prisoners were then transferred to their "cells," where they would remain under the supervision of "guards." Zimbardo equipped the guards with nightsticks, uniforms, and mirrored aviator sunglasses to prevent direct eye contact with the prisoners. Prisoners wore smocks, like hospital gowns, and stocking caps. Each was fitted with chains around one ankle and a number sewn onto their uniform. Guards were told to refer to each prisoner by number, not name.

Due to pressure from his girlfriend (later wife), and fearing the physical and mental health of his students, Zimbardo terminated his study early. He had intended the experiment to last two weeks. It lasted six days.

By day six, the situation had spiraled out of control: guards had become sadistic, subjecting prisoners to dangerous, psychological torture. Zimbardo himself got lost in the act. Taking on the role of superintendent, he permitted the abuse to continue and even participated alongside the guards to quell a prisoner revolt.

Thirty-three years later, Zimbardo testified in defense of a soldier being tried for the torture, assault, and abuse of detainees at Abu Ghraib prison in Iraq. Speaking from his own experience, Zimbardo argued for leniency. His judgment: situational pressures can result in inhumane misuses of power. Without proper training, limits, and supervision, average people can and often will abuse their authority over others. In fact, in the absence of any controls, this dynamic is highly probable. It's a dynamic inherent in the situation.

Zimbardo had gotten an answer to his question.

The Stanford Prison Experiment affirms our dimmest view of power, the view of power William Golding described in his dystopian novel *Lord of the Flies*. In that book, British schoolboys are stranded on a desert island without oversight or control, and regress into a terrifying contest between the powerful and their prey. This is the view of power that Thomas Hobbes also predicted, and which justified his argument for a strong government (in *Leviathan*) to protect the weak from the strong, and curtail the innate human drive for power, violence, and unrestrained personal gain.

These are not the only narratives of power—far from it. For every bleak *Lord of the Flies*, there is an uplifting story of a Harry Potter whose power of love and friendship triumphs over the power of evil. We revel in the stories of "people power" raising a nation out of colonialism, apartheid, and slavery. While there are Pol Pots and Joseph Stalins, there are also Mahatma Gandhis and Nelson Mandelas. There are totalitarian regimes, and also Velvet Revolutions; covertly funded military coups, and civil resistance movements spread from the "bottom up" through social media. There are selfish and unscrupulous CEOs as well as caring companies with a strong social consciousness, organizations that value their people and the planet as much as or above pure profit.

Zimbardo's experiment, however, seems to affirm Lord Acton's famous dictum: "Power tends to corrupt, and absolute power corrupts absolutely." But in light of these examples to the contrary, we should make a small correction. While power can corrupt absolutely, it doesn't corrupt *inevitably*. We can resist (and have resisted) its influence. Not every ruler is corrupt. Not every politician is corrupt. Not every rich person behaves badly.

The question about power worth investigating is not "why does power corrupt?" but "why does it *sometimes* corrupt, and sometimes not?" Why do we sometimes use power for self-serving reasons, while in other instances use it to further the common good? Why do some people succumb to power's venal effects and others don't? No doubt power has some corrupting influence. The questions are: how, to what degree, and when does it corrupt?

The three most common explanations for power's corrupting influence are **situational**, **dispositional**, and **psychosocial** theories. Zimbardo's view of power is **situational.** It states that the situation creates the condition for abuse of power.

The **dispositional** theory states that people's traits and characteristics create the tendency or likelihood to abuse power. Some personalities are simply more prone to abuse power. A growing body of literature suggests individuals with narcissistic or psychopathic personality disorders are drawn to leadership roles.[1] Their personality will manifest as dominating, abusive, charismatic, and controlling. Under the pressure of the situation, and tempted by opportunity, such a person will use their position to satisfy their personal needs to control and dominate.

While both theories account for some abuses of power, they don't take into consideration the diversity of leader behavior. Many people in high-ranking roles don't exhibit narcissistic or psychopathic tendencies. And not everyone is swayed to abuse their power in situations where abuses do occur. There needs to be another theory, somewhere between the situation and the personality. This is the **psychosocial** explanation, and recent experiments on the cognitive and affective influences of high power affirm its view.[2]

As we will learn later in this chapter, when researchers randomly assign participants high- or low-ranking roles, participants' behaviors and attitudes change. What's fascinating about these studies is that the same results occur despite very different personality traits tested. And the same results occur without dramatically manipulating the situation as Zimbardo did. In fact, researchers simply "primed" participants to identify with a high-ranking role.

"Priming" is a means of unconsciously activating an association or memory. In the studies I'll review in a few pages, researchers primed participants by asking them to remember a time when they felt powerful, or assigning the person a role with additional responsibility or privileges. The findings were fascinating: ordinary people, when primed to be in the high-rank role, display different attitudes and behaviors than the others, regardless of personality.

Psychosocial studies indicate it is the *role*, and not the personality, that carries traits we associate with poor leadership.[3] A role is a set of behaviors that carries social meaning. In sociology, roles are understood as the enactment of social expectations. A role can be

codified with a title such as CEO, professor, or doctor; or can also
be an informal enactment of behaviors, determined by the social
field—for instance, the role you play in your friendship or family
group (the nurturer, rebel, problem solver, et cetera). Roles belong to
a given social context, and we step in and out of them as we change
social settings. Thus, researchers are able to prime participants to
act in a role for the duration of an experiment.

This third, psychosocial theory looks at the intersection of the
person in the role: what happens to people as they step into a role
that carries power. The corrupting influence of power is not inherent in any one individual, and it's not inseparable from the situation.
Corruption is partly built into the role. It's both a psychological and
social phenomenon.

You probably already know roles are powerful. Think of what
people frequently say after becoming a parent for the first time: the
role has completely changed them. New parents display new attitudes,
new feelings, and even new behaviors. If you've ever been elected or
promoted into a role, or if you remember your first day in a job where
you had new responsibilities, you have felt the force of the role. Psychologist Arnold Mindell, whose theory of rank and group dynamics
rests on the concept of roles, says, "Roles...change rapidly because
they are a function of the moment and locality. Roles in groups are
not fixed but fluid. They are filled by different individuals and parties over time, keeping the roles in a constant state of flux."[4]

Robert Sutton, professor of organizational behavior at the Stanford University Graduate School of Business, has written exten-
sively about power and leadership. In an article for the *Harvard
Business Review*, Sutton describes how, as people step into a management role, they become susceptible to its blind spots. In "12 Things
Good Bosses Believe," Number 1 on Sutton's list is "I have a flawed
and incomplete understanding of what it's like to work for me."[5]

Sutton concludes with Number 12: "Because I wield power over others, I am at great risk of acting like an insensitive jerk—and not realizing it."

Lord Acton is right, in a sense: power corrupts. But it's the *role* of power that corrupts. This understanding shifts our common paradigm of power. Power is not only material, the result of having more money, social status, legal authority, or strength; it is a state of mind, an attitude, and a set of behaviors. Nor is power static, something you either have or lack. Rather, power is dynamic, intrinsically related to the roles we occupy, roles that are subject to the variations of context.

So, given this updated point of view, let's return to our original question: Why does power *sometimes* corrupt, and sometimes not? When, why, and whom does power corrupt?

Means, Motive, and Opportunity

Thanks to the popularity of crime shows on television, most of us know the expression "means, motive, and opportunity." In criminal law, in order to establish guilt, each must exist.

Means refers to ability: Is the culprit physically and psychologically able to commit the crime? Are they strong enough? Did they have a weapon?

Opportunity is time and place. Was the offender physically present, in the vicinity, at the time the crime was committed? Do they have an alibi?

Motive is the reason for committing the crime. Someone must need or want something. Most wrongdoers stand to gain something by committing a crime: Will they collect an inheritance or life insurance policy? Were they trying to get rid of the rich husband so they could run off together? Was it a revenge killing?

Means, motive, and opportunity also explain why, when, and whom power corrupts. Corruption happens when means, motive, and opportunity collide. One of the reasons why power is so nefarious is because *power provides the means and opportunity for its own abuse.*

The means of power are its psychosocial influences, the psychology of the high-ranking role. Something happens to us when we step into roles of power: it's like being under the influence of drugs or alcohol or having someone cast a magic spell that alters our perceptions and emotions. As though slipping on Sauron's Ring of Power, when we step into a position of power, we think, feel, and behave differently. The role itself allows for its own corruption. It is a magic that must be carefully managed.

Means alone are compelling enough, but they come coupled with opportunity. The opportunities of power are well known: the perks and privileges, the private parking spots and stretch limousines, the fame and fortune that tempt us. Opportunity is what law attempts to curtail, and the situational factors that Zimbardo documented in his experiment: reduced oversight, access to precious resources, limited accountability and the license to act with few checks or balances, and so on. Opportunity also includes other people's admiration and projections. When we are in a high-ranking role, people see us differently and adjust their behavior around us accordingly. The means of power—its psychosocial influences—are amplified and reinforced by these social factors, creating an ever-escalating, positive feedback loop, a veritable "perfect storm" for the misuse of power.

What about motive? What tempts us to cross that line, to take advantage of the means and opportunity? Why do some people take advantage of what power offers and others don't?

Indeed, **motive** is the key to explaining how we use power. People's emotional states and needs drive behavior, and thus motive is the linchpin, the chief focus of this *User's Guide.* We will address motive, in detail in the next chapter. Figure 1.1 shows how means, motive and opportunity operate, and the mutually enforcing influences of means and opportunity.

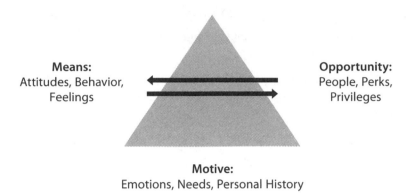

Figure 1.1

First, let's investigate the psychosocial and situational factors, the means and opportunity that contribute to power's corruptive effect. What are the psychosocial influences that make power corrupt? What strange spell is cast when we step into high-ranking roles?

Steve Jobs's Reality Distortion Field

Imagine you're attending the evening reception of your first professional conference. You walk into the soirée and see hundreds of people mingling in small groups, among them some of the big shots in your field. And there you are, standing at the entrance, by yourself, looking into that room of important strangers. You might hesitate a bit while scanning the crowd inside. Not far from view, you spy a buffet table with drinks, pamphlets, and flyers. You breathe a sigh of relief. You have somewhere to go and something to do with your hands.

Grasping your glass, and feeling a bit more confident, you turn from the table and see a group of people nearby who look interesting. You take a few steps in their direction, standing close enough to hear what they're saying, without looking too eager to join. You wait for a gap in the conversation or a shift in their bodies to make room for you.

This whole time, your social antennae have been actively scanning the surroundings, reading the nonverbal signals that allow you to adjust your behavior to fit the social context. Your low social rank in that setting makes you acutely aware of and sensitive to the slightest reactions and social nuances of others.

Now switch the scene around: same conference, only now, you're the big shot in the room, maybe the keynote speaker. From this vantage point, your body would move very differently. You'd enter the room with less uncertainty. Because you're the keynote speaker, you don't have to worry about approaching people. They'd approach you. They'd ask you questions and eagerly wait for your signals. Their expectant looks would encourage you to speak. This time around, your social antennae may be just as active as they would be if you had less rank, but now, in your higher-ranking role, you don't have to adjust to others; they adjust to you.

We don't need to attend conferences to recognize this dynamic. It happens all the time: at parties, work, and neighborhood gatherings. When you're an insider, you adjust yourself less to others. You are more accepted or sought after, and your perception of your status is reflected in your nonverbal signals and the signals of those around you.

The reverse is true as well: being uncertain and having low rank is communicated in signals of hesitance, caution, and hyper-sensitivity.

The conference example highlights one of the ways high-ranking roles influence reality. Power is more than the force to *do*: to impact, influence, and empower. It's also the freedom to *not do*: to not fit in, not adapt, and not feel pressured by others. Power gives us immunity from social expectations.

Dacher Keltner and his colleagues Cameron Anderson (of the University of California Berkeley) and Deborah Gruenfeld (of Stanford) conducted a series of experiments in which they randomly assigned individuals high- and low-power roles to see what, and if any, differences in behavior and attitude emerged. What Keltner, Anderson, and

Gruenfeld found is that those in the high-ranking roles were less socially inhibited, acted in self-serving ways, and took up more space and more time in conversation. These high-power individuals were more attuned to their inner states and feelings, more inclined to follow their ideas than be influenced by others'.[6] The researchers referred to this set of behaviors as *disinhibition*.

As humans, we can sense disinhibition without having to read the research. We make fun of leaders for their eccentricity, egotism, and self-importance. We love stories about the extravagant and out-rageous antics of the rich and famous. What's different about the research conducted by Keltner et al. is that it turns conventional wisdom upside down. We typically see the disinhibited behavior of leaders as a preexisting condition. We think narcissists are drawn to high-ranking roles to indulge their disorder. But research shows that power *bestows* disinhibition. When conditions can be manipulated to create arbitrary power differentials between people of equal status, the same behavior surfaces.

In an earlier experiment by Keltner and another colleague, three undergraduates were told they were participating in a study of atti-tudes on social issues.[7] They were really participating in a study of power. Keltner and his team broke participants into groups of three and asked each group to discuss a controversial social issue and then write policy recommendations about it. Before they started, one of the three members of each group was chosen at random to evaluate the other two and assign points on their performance. The points affected members' chances of winning a prize after the experiment. This act of priming for power ensured that there were real conse-quences for the one person in the high-ranking role.

After about thirty minutes, one of the facilitators of the experi-ment brought the group a plate of five cookies. With five cookies shared among three people, there would be enough to go around: each person could take one cookie without any awkwardness. But that left two cookies for three people. Taking a second cookie meant someone got only one. So, who do you think was more likely to reach for a second cookie at the expense of someone else? Those assigned to be evaluators not only ate the second cookie far more often, but they also ate it with greater abandon; they chewed the cookies with their mouths open, and spewed crumbs all over themselves and on the table.[8]

Steve Jobs, Apple's founder and former CEO, was a famously and flagrantly disinhibited leader. He drove without license plates. He parked his car in spaces reserved for handicapped drivers. He didn't wear shoes, and for years, didn't "believe" in bathing. He routinely challenged his engineers to meet unreasonable deadlines and solve impossible design problems. Bud Tribble, the manager of the original Macintosh software development team, called it Jobs's "reality distortion field," which he defined as Jobs's "eagerness to bend any fact to fit the purpose at hand."[9] Jobs enjoyed the ultimate disinhibition: reality didn't faze him.

What function, if any, does disinhibition serve? Leaders, entrepreneurs, social activists, and creative types like Steve Jobs need disinhibition. Think of revolutionaries like Martin Luther King Jr., Albert Einstein, Oprah Winfrey, and Eleanor Roosevelt—people who changed industries, challenged the status quo, transformed society, and ignored impossible odds. They were all disinhibited to a degree. To do something that's never been done before means thinking outside the frontiers of social convention. You can't be creative or revolutionary while concerned with what others think. You need to be able to brush aside traditional wisdom, value your subjective feelings, and take risks others don't or can't take.

Leaders need disinhibition to make difficult decisions in a sea of social pressures. Without immunity from others' expectations, leaders suffer from "paralysis by analysis," overly concerned with making the right decision—or the one that pleases the most people. Disinhibition allows power users to act decisively when necessary, even when they lack all the pertinent information.

While disinhibition can revolutionize an industry, it can also leave a trail of destruction in its wake. Disinhibited conduct is also the annoying behavior we see in persons of power who interrupt, dominate conversations, and patronize others. So-called "mansplaining" and "manspreading" behaviors attributed to men are disinhibited actions of high status: taking up too much space, explaining things in a condescending manner, and believing they can weigh in on matters beyond the boundaries of their knowledge. These behaviors can be annoying, but disinhibition can be much worse—it can also result in socially inappropriate behavior, criminal activity, and even sexual harassment.

The ability to act without regard to convention is a magic that must be carefully managed. And yet this magic is strengthened and amplified by another, closely allied, and equally potent psychological effect of power: illusory control.

"Trust me. I know what I'm doing."

On October 4, 1973, Zvi Samir, chief of Mossad—the Israeli Intelligence Agency—received a report that Soviet advisors and their families had left Egypt and Syria. The night before, intelligence sources showed Samir aerial photographs of larger-than-normal concentrations of artillery on the Egyptian and Syrian borders. The next day, he received a cable from a source in the U.S. surveillance community warning him that an attack on Israel was imminent.

Alarmed by this trifecta of troubling information, Samir brought his concerns to the heads of state. But Eli Zeira, director of Israel's military intelligence, dismissed Samir's evidence with a wave of his hand.

"There will be no war," Zeira pronounced with complete confidence. He had put his faith in a theory, popular at the time, that Syria wouldn't attack without Egypt's co-signature, and Egypt wasn't planning to go to war before 1975. Even when King Hussein of Jordan personally called Israeli Prime Minister Golda Meir and warned her to prepare for an Egyptian-Syrian assault, Zeira convinced her and other officials not to worry. We now know how wrong he was, of course. Two days later, on Yom Kippur, Egypt and Syria "surprised" Israel with an attack, initiating what is now called the Yom Kippur War.

Looking back, Zeira's arrogance seems astounding, as does the willingness of the Israeli heads of state to follow him. Yet, their error is but one of the thousands of stories of leaders throughout history flagrantly underestimating the costs and consequences of their decisions, and overestimating their chances of success. From the captain of the Titanic, who ignored warnings of icebergs, to Napoleon invading Russia in winter, to George W. Bush and Secretary of Defense Donald Rumsfeld proclaiming the war in Iraq would last no more than six weeks,[10] leaders notoriously underestimate risks and overestimate the potential for success.

We tend to see these gross exaggerations as politically motivated. They may be, but they are also the psychological effects of power. Studies demonstrate that regular people, when primed to have higher status, begin to believe they can control events, including those outside their sphere of influence. Researchers Nathanael Fast, Deborah Gruenfeld and others have linked high power to *illusory control*: the belief in one's ability to influence outcomes that are beyond one's reach, even outcomes determined by chance, such as rolling dice.[11] In one experiment, Gruenfeld and Fast primed participants to have high power, low power, or be in the baseline group, and told participants they would be rewarded with a cash prize for correctly guessing the results of a single roll of a six-sided die. They gave participants the choice of rolling the die themselves, or having a researcher roll it for them. The researchers assumed those in the high-power group would more likely choose to roll the die themselves, believing themselves to have greater control over the outcome. In fact, 100% of those primed in the high-power role chose to roll the die themselves, in contrast to only 58% of those in the low-power role.

Actually, a belief in your ability to have influence over events is adaptive. It's a useful, even healthy trait. Psychologists call it an *internal locus of control,* the extent to which individuals believe they can positively impact the outcome of things through their own efforts and abilities. Studies that survey the effect of attitudes on health show that when someone has an internalized locus of control, they have better health outcomes. Optimism and self-esteem are correlated with the ability to handle stress and adversity, whereas the absence of perceived control is linked to depression, pessimism, and withdrawal from challenging situations.[12]

The belief that you can handle whatever arises is essential to good leadership, not just good health. An internal locus of control allows you to be more confident in your decisions and to take bold action when necessary. Entrepreneurs display higher-than-average amounts of confidence and optimism. Though it's widely known that two-thirds of all businesses fail in their first five years, eighty percent of entrepreneurs believe their ventures will succeed. Even when shown the statistics, they remain optimistic.

Thank goodness, says psychologist and Nobel laureate Daniel Kahneman.[13] Kahneman, who wrote the bestseller *Thinking Fast and Slow,* explains, "Delusions, to a certain extent, are helpful." In fact, "A lot of progress in the world is driven by delusional optimism."

It's not just entrepreneurs who have delusional optimism. Inventors and leaders rate high in this cognitive error. As Kahneman says, "We want to be led by people who believe it's going to be OK. Optimists are likely to be more successful because they will inspire optimism in others."

Like disinhibition, for every upside there is a downside. An illusory sense of control, as we have witnessed, allows leaders to start wars, ignore intelligence, and underestimate risk. And it also leads them to believe they can get away with fraud, adultery, and other malfeasance while in the public eye. Bill Clinton, even as Paula Jones was suing him for sexual harassment, believed he could conduct a clandestine affair with Monica Lewinsky. Lance Armstrong believed he could conceal his doping from authorities and investigators by threatening and coercing team directors, and doctors, and other cyclists. Former United States Representative Anthony Weiner sent nude photos and sexually explicit messages on Twitter and Facebook, believing, incredibly, none of his pictures would come to light. None of these ethical lapses was caused by an illusory sense of control, but each person's belief they could get away with it was. In each case, a powerful person believed they could control the future and paid a steep price for the error.

Immunity from social pressure and norms, accompanied by the confidence you can influence things outside your control, is a potent mix. Along with disinhibition and a sense of illusory control, a third influence enters the mix: diminished interest in and feelings for others, especially those with lower rank.

"Let them eat cake."

There is no proof that Marie Antoinette ever uttered those words upon learning the peasants in her country had no bread to eat. But we remember and repeat the phrase because it perfectly captures the stereotype of the callous and clueless ruler. From the hotelier Leona Helmsley, the so-called "Queen of Mean," to "Chainsaw Al" Dunlop, the CEO and professional downsizer who fired thousands of employees and closed down plants and factories, we have no short-age of tales of cold-hearted leaders. Alan Dershowitz, the famous lawyer, recounts one especially egregious anecdote about Helmsley: as the two of them sat discussing legal strategy over breakfast at one of her hotels, their waiter brought over a cup of tea that had a little water spilled in the saucer. Helmsley became outraged. She threw the cup and saucer onto the floor and ordered the waiter to get on his hands and knees to beg for his job.[14]

Helmsley's purported behavior may seem extreme, but it demonstrates how high rank diminishes empathy. More accurately, high status and power impede our ability to take on another's perspective.[15] In psychology, perspective-taking is an important way humans create and maintain social bonds. The ability to put oneself in another's shoes is a key social skill, critical for making friends, maintaining intimacy, and resolving conflict. And yet, those with high rank and power do this poorly.[16] Actually, we all do it more poorly when given even a little "crumb" of rank. As Mindell says, bluntly, high social rank makes us unconscious of others.[17]

Research by Columbia Business School psychology professor Adam Galinsky and his colleagues demonstrates that people with higher rank are less able to judge others' emotions accurately, and yet give themselves high ratings on their ability to do so.[18] In one of Galinsky's studies, participants were shown photographs of people's faces displaying different emotions, such as happiness, fear, anger, and sadness. Participants were asked to name the emotions they saw. It should come as no surprise that those in a high-ranking role got the answer wrong a greater number of times than the participants who had not been primed.

This research confirms what we intuitively feel: people in high power are less empathic. From supervisors to parents, people at the top pay less attention to others and don't consider others' perspectives. When they do pay attention, it's usually for their own purposes or needs, as is the case for Miranda Priestly, the demanding boss in *The Devil Wears Prada*, who calls every assistant "Emily" simply because that's the name she remembers. To a person in a high-ranking role, people become "instrumental"—a means to an end, important to us only insofar as they give us what we need.

Can there be any value at all in reduced empathy? It's a conspicuously ugly trait of power. What could it accomplish besides bullying?

But consider this: if, when leading a group of people, we were too greatly affected by each person's circumstances, it would be extremely difficult to make decisions for the whole. It's much harder to fire people when you think of them as individuals with families and loved ones, when you feel responsible for their well-being.

Sometimes, the greater good of our group, community, family, or organization overrides individual needs. Consider the facilitator who is overly concerned with each individual participant's needs. Taking every question, listening to each person's idea, and soliciting the group's input about which activities to do next plunges the group into chaos. When a teacher or team leader doesn't help guide what happens, members engage in conflict with each other. Unbridled democracy produces conflict: people are seldom deciding in terms of what's best for the group's learning or development, speaking up instead with their own personal preferences.

Even families often sacrifice one relative's needs to meet the shared interests of everyone else. Consider the choices of sending aged relatives to nursing homes because of the inconvenience and difficulty of caring for them in one's home, or the family that isolates their autistic and aggression-prone son from his sister's birthday party. In either scenario, the family members making the decision—the ones in power—face a tough call. They may tell themselves it was the best option available, the only solution they had. And they may be right. Caring for the well-being of each member is a luxury leaders cannot always afford.

Given these psychological influences—decreased inhibition, illusory control, and decreased empathy for others—we begin to see why power is so corruptive. These psychological influences are the means of power: they alter us in ways that make abusing power possible. However, while these means exist in our minds, they also derive from a social field. Interaction with our community enforces and amplifies our attitudes, behaviors, and feelings about others.

Figure 1.1 showed how means come with and are reinforced by opportunity, the perks, privileges, and people surrounding a high-ranking role. We've just reviewed the *means*, on the left side of the triangle, the psychological influences of disinhibition, illusory control, and decreased empathy. Let's take another look, taking into account some of the *opportunities* high power bestows. The next section will explore some of the challenges on the right side of the triangle, the corrupting opportunities power conveys: self-fulfilling prophecies, lack of feedback, and lack of role conflict.

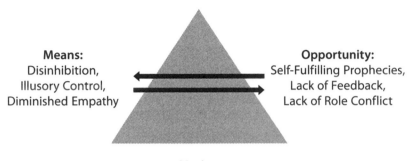

Means:
Disinhibition,
Illusory Control,
Diminished Empathy

Opportunity:
Self-Fulfilling Prophecies,
Lack of Feedback,
Lack of Role Conflict

Motive:
Emotions, Feelings, Personal History

Figure 1.2

Self-Fulfilling Prophecies and Positive Feedback Loops

In the 1979 movie *Being There*, Chance, a mentally disabled and illiterate gardener who has lived on his employer's estate his whole life, suddenly finds himself homeless and rudderless after the death of his employer. His only knowledge of the world is what he's seen on television. Lacking direction, Chance wanders outside the walls of the protected estate for the first time in his life, entering a strange and unfamiliar world. Through a series of coincidental and fantastical encounters, he meets a woman who—judging from his fancy clothes (he was dressed in his former employer's suit)—takes him to be an educated, wealthy man. Her initial snap judgment colors everything he does and says. No matter how senseless or ignorant his statements are, she ascribes them profound wisdom and keen insight. In an escalating feedback loop, with each encounter confirming others' impressions, Chance, now called "Chauncey Gardiner," ultimately winds up advising the president of the United States.

Some months later, Louise, the black housekeeper who worked for "Chauncey's" employer—and cared for Chance in his boyhood—is watching television and spots a familiar face. Astounded and flabbergasted to see Chance in the news, she turns to the audience and says:

> It's for sure a white man's world in America. Look here: I raised that boy since he was the size of a pissant. And I'll say right now, he never learned to read and write. No, sir—had no brains at all. Was stuffed with rice pudding between the ears. Shortchanged by the Lord, and dumb as a jackass. Look at him now! Yessir, all you've got to be is white in America to get whatever you want.

Louise is right. Other people's expectations and perceptions define our status, shape our performance, and determine our success. Studies frequently show that high rank (and low rank) is not just something a person holds, but a quality that lives in the minds of those around you. As I mentioned earlier, rank belongs to the role, and others' perceptions reify our rank. People treat a leader like a leader simply because she "fits the bill." Conversely, we treat people poorly when they fit negative stereotypes. Positive expectations of others furnish us with the benefit of the doubt, while their negative judgments and expectations stand in the way of our success.

When we're viewed through a positive lens, our mistakes and shortcomings are either ignored, explained away, or simply brushed off as anomalies. We think the leader is smart *because* she's the leader. If she makes a mistake, we're likely to dismiss it as a one-off exception. And when she says something that contradicts our beliefs, we're likely to change our minds to conform to a pre-existing bias about her intelligence. As in the fable "The Emperor's New Clothes," it is almost impossible for us to break through our collective, hypnotic belief in the leader's greatness.

You might recognize this virtuous circle as a *self-fulfilling prophecy*: people's expectations cause an outcome that confirms their expectations. Robert Merton, the famous sociologist, first wrote about the self-fulfilling prophecy in his classic book *Social Theory and Social Structure*. Merton and others' research shows that advantage creates the condition for more advantage. Or, to put it another way: the more you have, the more you get.[19] More rewards and resources go to those whom others perceive favorably: those in high-power positions and those with high status.[20]

Merton researched the career paths of fellow scientists and found that those with higher status earned disproportionately greater resources (money, access to research assistants, lower teaching loads allowing for more productivity, equipment, laboratories, speaking engagements) because of their reputation, and thus received more grants, rewards, and top positions in their fields.[21] The same phenomenon occurs across fields: graduates from prestigious law schools have more opportunities to try big cases than graduates from lesser-known institutions.

Of course, the reverse is true as well. Disadvantage creates conditions for further disadvantages. Women, people of color, and other disadvantaged groups not only face discriminatory practices, but if and when people from these groups are admitted into jobs or universities, they also have to succeed against people's preconceived assessment of their abilities. Stereotypical judgments create negative expectations of someone's competency. An individual from a socially marginalized group gets fewer opportunities to advance, and that person's failure to attain high-profile tasks or roles confirms the widely held belief in their group's incompetence.

Several studies in recent years demonstrate how these beliefs, commonly referred to as "unconscious bias," influence advancement. In one study, a participant team of "interviewers" evaluated résumés. When the name on the résumé was a common white name, the applicant was 50% more likely to get an interview compared to applicants with common black names—even when the qualifications were the same and the résumés identical.[22] Looking into gender bias in science careers, a recent study showed both female and male faculty rated male students more highly than female students, even when their applications were identical.[23]

Self-fulfilling prophecies confirming higher status are one of the reasons many leaders secretly feel fraudulent: they sense that people's judgments are unmoored from reality. The accolades, opportunities, and admiration *are* sometimes undeserved. When leaders become promoted beyond their level of competency, they either "drink the Kool-Aid" and believe in their greatness, or develop "imposter syndrome," unable to feel ownership over their accomplishments.

Here's the danger: either belief creates a motive for leaders to hide their mistakes, disguise their incompetence, and refuse to seek help or advice to keep up the façade. They're afraid to tarnish the image in others' minds. The frightening possibility raised is that, in a high-ranking role, we're living in a sort of "deprivation chamber," devoid of honest feedback and propped up by images and expectations disconnected from real data.

It's Lonely At the Top

They say it's lonely at the top. It's not just lonely; it's quiet, too. Eerily quiet. The power a leader wields over her subordinates' careers makes underlings reluctant to give honest feedback. The leader frequently has a trusted inner circle of advisors who themselves have a stake in the game. They may feel intimidated by the leader's rank and tell her only what they think she wants to hear. Or, afraid to irritate her, they may minimize or hide bad news. It could also be that they have their own ambitions for her job—their own agendas—so they spin information to serve their interests.

It's lonely at the top because the higher you rise the more dependent you are on others for information. Everything gets filtered up to you through layers of staff, advisors, and members of your inner circle. And as you gain leverage, you lose social contacts. This is a both a perk and peril of power. In a high-ranking role, you don't have to run your errands or do your own menial tasks. You get to call the time and place of meetings or, if you wish, skip them altogether. When you have higher rank, you can pick and choose to whom you relate.

One reason it's so lonely at the top is simple: your high rank results in less *role conflict*. Role conflict is the stress we have when two or more roles compete for our time and attention. Role conflict is a constant for many women as they try to juggle family, work, friends, and self-care. The fewer roles we have to navigate, the less role conflict, and the more we're able to focus on in the moment. The less divergent our list of responsibilities is, the more time we can spend in our one, high-ranking role.

Sounds good, right? But there's a cost to reducing role conflict.

Shifting constantly in and out of high- and low-ranking roles benefits our emotional and social development. In struggling over the needs of different roles, we are forced to imagine what others feel. We wrestle with guilt and loyalty: Should we go to the parent–teacher conference at school, or visit our mother who just got out of surgery? Should we stay late and review the reports for tomorrow's big presentation, or go home and cook soup for our friend who's going through chemotherapy? We're in and out of the others' shoes, pulled back and forth between our feelings for others and our self-interest. It helps us develop empathy and insight into others.

In fact, being in low-ranking roles allows us to navigate our high-ranking positions better. Power is such a sought-after commodity that we tend to overlook the immense value of low-ranking roles, positions in which we feel less powerful. As you read earlier in this chapter, low rank socially attunes us, forcing us to develop our relationship abilities. When we don't have easy access to resources, we rely on our connections with others. The ability to reach out to others and have healthy and sustained interpersonal relationships is a fundamental skill set. These skills and sub-skills begin in infancy: vulnerability, kindness and empathy, cooperation and sharing, and the courage to reach out—risking rejection and the possibility of conflict.

A powerful role, on the other hand, can be a shortcut to all that hard work. We can limit our interactions, listening only to those who ratify our high rank. Admiration and sycophancy masquerade as friendship or intimacy. If we have trouble making friends or find intimacy difficult, our high-ranking role can be a quick route to relationships. Staying in a high-ranking role means we don't have to exercise that relationship muscle much, and thus we don't develop the courage to risk rejection or loneliness. If you have something others want, you have control over them.

Both high- and low-ranking roles are part of our social selves. Either vantage point shows us a different window into the world. A low-ranking role gives us more empathy and insight to others' struggles. The high-ranking role gives us the opportunity to lead and have influence. The conflict between roles increases our overall relational abilities, broadens our perspective of ourselves in the environment, and increases our self-awareness.

Self-fulfilling prophecies, lack of genuine feedback, and lack of role conflict are some of the less obvious and yet very significant influences of opportunity. Alongside these influences lay highly valued assets and temptations that can lead directly to corruption —things like money, classified information, personnel records, and social networks.

Summary

In this chapter, we've explored how power, like magic, has properties that can be used for good or bad. The *means* of power, the influences of a high-ranking role, give us greater immunity from social pressures, allow us to act in a more disinhibited fashion, and make us more enamored with our own ideas and less open to feedback. Our sense of control over events is heightened, as is our confidence in predicting positive outcomes. We show less empathy towards others, are less able to judge their emotions, and are less willing to take on their perspectives.

Opportunity, the social circumstances of our high-power role, amplifies these cognitive changes. We become subject to the self-fulfilling expectations of others when surrounded by subordinates and followers dependent on our approval. Isolation and lack of role conflict rob us of opportunities to grow our social and emotional intelligence.

Finally, the tangible perks of power round out authority's "perfect storm": access to money, resources, and information, all coupled with lax oversight and absent accountability.

It's no wonder people abuse power. But still we face the question: Why do some abuse power while others don't?

The truth is most people do *not* abuse their power. Most people are conscientious, ethical, and socially minded, and do not abuse their power. The real questions we need to examine are why, given the opportunity, do we sometimes take advantage of these conditions, and other times don't? What compels us to use our power in ways that misuse it? Why do we sometimes fail in our leadership roles, getting derailed by our personal needs, and forgetting to place the interests of our employees, students, customers, children, and clients above our own?

In the next chapter we will take a closer look at power and motive. What gives us motive and makes us corruptible? We'll explore how our personal stories intersect with our rank, and what we can we do to resist the pull of motive.

2

Motive:
What Makes People Corruptible?

It is weakness rather than wickedness
which renders men unfit to be trusted with unlimited power.
—JOHN ADAMS

At 7:45am I looked out on a sea of yawning, bored 10th graders and reconsidered my career choice. It was 1979. I was twenty years old and starting my first day as a student teacher. The four years between my age and my students', a chasm that had felt lengthy enough the day before, seemed to have dramatically shrunk. Now, looking into those skeptical faces, I started to wonder if 5th graders would have been less intimidating. I caught a few of the students sneaking looks at each other, and I knew they thought the same.

That morning was one of my biggest lessons in the laws of power. I saw, or rather, felt what my hard-earned teaching degree really meant in the classroom. That piece of paper for which I had paid—and was paying—a fortune didn't translate into the power to enact my role. To make it through that first hour, and win them over, I had to draw on every trait, trick, and instinct I had. That was when I realized the inherent frailty of *positional power*. Positional power put me in front of the class.

But I needed something else, something like my own *personal power*, if I were to survive that hour.

Three months later, at the end of my student-teaching stint, I learned my second lesson in power: on my last day, I retrieved from my mailbox a manila envelope filled with feedback forms my students had filled out. I stuffed the envelope in my bag and walked back to campus. I had a meeting that afternoon with my advisor. While I waited outside his office, I leafed through the forms, and as I read each one, a smile spread over my face: lots of nice feedback, lots of comments appreciating my friendly and open style. Then, suddenly, the smile evaporated—I felt like I had been punched in the stomach.

I think you played favorites, one student wrote. I can still see the small, scrawling handwriting to this day. Though no one else could see me, my face grew hot. I turned beet-red, feeling ashamed and embarrassed.

I knew exactly who had written the comment.

Way in the back, in the far right corner of the classroom, had sat the only two African American girls in the school. They always sat together, and they seldom participated in class. When I called on them, they rarely responded with more than an "I dunno." I felt daunted and inept. I didn't know how to engage them. Whenever the class worked alone at their desks, I would walk over to the two and check in. I would ask each how it was going, but neither looked up or said anything. I was at a loss—I didn't know what to do.

So I did something that shames me to this day. I did nothing. I let the issue slide by. As the semester progressed, I would call on them less and less. I never sought help from my advisor, never talked to the classroom teacher about it, and never asked to speak with them privately or offer support in private. I failed to move beyond my own limitations. Of course I knew about racial inequity at the time, and of the challenge these students must have been facing. I knew I had to do something, but I didn't. I was caught off guard by my feelings of inadequacy and I abdicated my higher rank and its responsibilities. I succumbed to feeling weak, and didn't challenge myself to put the students' needs and rights ahead of my feelings.

When we think about the abuse of power, what often comes to mind are the atrocities that horrify us: the genocides of Hitler, Stalin, or Pol Pot; the cold indifference of an institution that covers up sexual abuse; the extravagant excess of corporate fraud; the hypocritical corruption of politicians. But most abuses of power don't make it to the headlines. Most are the inadvertent acts, or corrupt uses of our power. Corruption implies a breach of the law, an illegal act. But it also refers to non-conscious, unintended, unpremeditated acts that break or stretch social and relational bonds, and in so doing, inflict harm. A better way to describe them might be "rank fouls." By and large, these are unconscious actions carried out by someone with high rank, good intentions, and benign neglect.

Since Freud first wrote about the superego, ego, and id, we've known of the gap between thought and action, between our espoused values and motives and what we actually manifest. We are far less conscious of ourselves than we like to admit. Back then, in the classroom, if you had asked me if I was deliberately ignoring my responsibilities, I would have acted defensively. I would have justified myself by describing my countless attempts to reach the girls and my genuine concern for their welfare. But my self-awareness was insufficient to close the gap between what I thought I was doing and what I actually did—and how it impacted them.

What I did as a twenty-year-old student teacher was a misuse of power. At least, to me, it was a misuse. Whether it was a *misuse* or an *abuse*, however, is not for me—the one with higher rank—to decide. From the perspective of those sixteen-year-olds, the only two racial minorities in that class in a small Ohio town, trying to get an education, it was probably, truly, an abuse of power.

And so it happens: average people misuse power daily in what appears to be trivial ways, and yet their actions can leave harmful, lasting effects on the target of their behavior.

This is the everyday misuse of power that makes our lives difficult. They are "rank fouls," like foul plays in sports, behaviors that are often unconscious or unintended—the results of a lapse in judgment, or anxiety, or fear, or ineptitude, or impetuousness. Sometimes they are also deliberate behaviors, such as neglecting duties, covering up inadequacies, or serving our self-interests.

The Trap of Feeling Powerless

Of all the misuses of power I've witnessed, almost all typically stem from a feeling of *powerlessness*. Like me, in that classroom, allowing my inadequacy get the better of me, most people in power are quick to admit to a *lack of power*.

I see this everywhere:

- Senior Vice Presidents complain about how difficult it is to talk to the CEO.
- CEOs struggle to work with their executive teams.
- Executive Directors feel thwarted by their boards, or by regulatory agencies.
- Teachers struggle to control the classroom.
- A doctor rushes through informing her patient of bad news because she's afraid of his emotional response.
- The mayor complains the media unfairly portrays her.
- A boss avoids intervening in a staff dispute, paralyzed by his fear of conflict.

It's not only leaders who fail to connect with their power. Parents feel overwhelmed and harried. The oldest child protests her unfair punishment for fighting, while her younger sibling (who started it) gets away without reprimand.

Those born into great social privilege complain that the inequities and hardships they face don't receive nearly as much attention as those inequities faced by people with less social privilege. A white person will dispute the existence of racism by pointing to the gains made by people of color. A man will disavow feminism by equating it with "man-hating," or citing instances of underreported sexual violence perpetuated against men. In each instance, one group disavows their advantage, and doubles down on their sense of powerlessness.

John Adams famously said, "It is weakness rather than wickedness which renders men unfit to be trusted with unlimited power." Weakness is a chief motive for misusing power. Feeling weak or fraudulent makes us hide our incompetence, fake our knowledge, or go into denial. Or, feeling cornered and defenseless, we lash out and attack. This is the fatal mismatch that accounts for a great deal of power misuse: the gap between the power we feel and the power we have, between our self-perceived sense of power and our objective power.

The gap is the focus of this chapter, for it is the distance between what others see and what we feel that creates the complexity and conflicts underlying how we use power. Specifically, *our inner sense of weakness or low rank results in ineffective and poor uses of power.*

Allow me to repeat that, because it is a fundamental and seemingly illogical truth about power. Our inner sense of weakness or low rank results in ineffective and poor uses of power. *Power is only powerful when we feel it.*

Throughout my career, it's always puzzled me: If power is so highly valued, how can it be that when we are in a high-ranking role we still feel weak—even powerless? Why do my executive coaching clients feel thwarted, fearful, and frustrated? Why don't people of privilege gratefully and happily admit their good fortune? Why did I feel so weak in front of that classroom, given my positional authority? This is the million-dollar question we need to explore: If high power is what we chase, why doesn't the powerful role protect us from the feelings of low rank?

Power and Context

A client of mine, Chandra, is the Chief Marketing Officer for a Fortune 500 technology company. She loves public speaking, and is a sought-after keynote speaker at the top technology conferences in the world. But whenever she's around her boss, the CEO, Chandra becomes tongue-tied. She feels much more comfortable speaking to a room of five hundred strangers than to her boss in a one-on-one meeting. Something about his style makes her feel stupid, and she has trouble presenting her ideas with force and confidence. He is a "numbers guy" and no matter how much she prepares the numbers, she still gets rattled and feels incompetent. She does much better speaking extemporaneously, but that style doesn't cut it when it comes to data.

I once had a colleague whom we'll call Luis. Luis was an assistant professor of political science and was extremely popular with students. Most students. He also had more complaints lodged against him than other professors. As the child of migrant workers, Luis was highly sensitive to topics regarding immigration. When something hit close to home, his voice rose, his face turned red, and he pounded his fist on the lectern. He once kicked a student out of his class after she said she thought immigrants should speak English as a precondition to entering the country.

Chandra and Luis have high positional power, but in certain situations, they lose their *feelings* of power. The two situations—speaking with the boss, the topic of immigration—lower Luis' and Chandra's self-perceived power. This is the problem with social power, the power that comes from our position or social status: the power of your role doesn't transfer into a feeling of power in every situation. *Social power doesn't always feel powerful.*

How and why can situations change our sense of power? Think of each situation, or context, as a country. In every country, there is a local "currency" based on what's valued. In a country with no printed money, currency would be the goods people traded. For instance, in my local "country" of Oregon, if I wanted to trade water for food, well, here in the rain-soaked Pacific Northwest, I wouldn't have much bargaining power. There's too much water here for it to be highly valued. But if I had a tanning booth and others traded food for hours in the booth, well, I'd have plenty to eat! In fact, I might be rich. The context, the rainy Pacific Northwest in this case, determines what is of value—what we value.

The same holds true for power. Each context has a different set of values, determined by the constellation of people, customs, issues, and dynamics present. Chandra's boss is a "numbers" guy; he values data, numbers, and metrics. Chandra is more of a "big picture" people person; she values ideas, communication, and relationships. But he's the boss, so she has to use his "currency," a currency of which she has less.

Context is determined by topic and task, not just people. For Luis, for instance, the topic of immigration changes the context to an extent: from classroom to political debate. I can relate. In the classroom, for me as a student teacher, the different tasks changed the context and rendered me unable. As long as the task required me to speak about facts and knowledge, I felt powerful. I had the skills that were valued for that task. But when the task changed from imparting knowledge to one-to-one advising, across a gulf of race, as I needed to do with those girls, so too did the context. At the age of twenty, I possessed fewer of the skills needed for the more emotionally challenging task of advising. Hence, my sense of power dropped.

Changing context changes something in us. Every environment contains different people, different topics, and different norms that determine valued resources, styles, and behavior.

Many years ago, I was part of a team working with trade union leaders on an enterprise development project in the former Yugoslavian Republic of Macedonia. It had only been a few years since the collapse of communism in the country, and our project was to support the transition to a free market economy.

My task during this phase of the project was to facilitate a series of day-long seminars with the trade union presidents, helping them design the enterprise development programs for their workers. That was the designated topic, but in the background simmered other issues—issues that began to obstruct our progress.

Early one morning, as we tried to tackle the topic of program trainers' per diem rates, the simmering issues came to full boil. They balked at our proposed rates. I should have known better, but I got annoyed. It was the 1990s, and the economy of Macedonia had contributed to the highest unemployment rate in Europe. There were precious few opportunities for income, and the per diem rates we were offering were higher than their daily salary. How could they not be happy with this opportunity?

Conflict erupted. My colleague and I were ill-prepared for it. The topic switched from program design to economic inequity, the power differential between Western Europe and former Communist countries in Eastern Europe, and the unconscious paternalism underlying development efforts and international aid.

The topic of money shifted the dynamics of our conversation, and so too our sense of power. Occupying our same roles, talking to the same people we had training, we were unable to successfully facilitate the conflict. We knew we could handle enterprise development, but not the topic of economic inequity between our countries. Imperceptibly, the context had shifted.

The topic of money switched the footing during that seminar, catching us off guard, and dropping our leadership abilities in that moment. The topic of immigration tripped a wire inside for Luis, and plunged him back to childhood, back to feelings of injustice. As the context changed, so too did his role, from professor to social activist. The topic trumped his higher social rank as his emotions took over. While his sense of power plummeted, his objective power remained the same. From the inside, he *felt* himself to be a member of an oppressed group, fighting injustice. From the outside, however, his students perceived an angry, intimidating teacher berating them.

When the topic of economic inequity came to the surface during the seminar with labor leaders in Macedonia, my status as consultant dropped considerably, as I was unprepared and unable to facilitate the dialogue. When I was required to hold a difficult conversation as the student teacher, my self-perceived power dropped like a stone. My unconsciousness of racism, my fear of making a mistake, and my desire to be liked all collided to freeze me in my tracks and deplete my feelings of power.

In these examples, Luis, Chandra, my colleague and I didn't lose our positional power; we lost access to our *feelings* of power. Power is more than an objective assignment of position, or the possession of status. *Power is a state of mind.*

Perhaps because it's difficult to see a person's complexity, perhaps because power tends to dazzle us, it's easy to forget that people with high rank also have emotions. They too feel vulnerable, hurt, defensive, or scared. Feelings are critical to our use of power, because how we feel drives our behavior.[1] When the roles have power, but the people occupying them don't feel it, for whatever reason, they are at risk of using their power poorly. They struggle to keep other people's or the organization's interests at heart, and instead, serve their own emotional interests.

The Threat of Low Rank

It's important, yet also amazing, how seriously feelings of weakness affect how we use our power. Some of my colleagues who work as diversity and inclusion educators joke about the "race to the margins," and the "Oppression Olympics": who can claim the lowest rank status? Whose oppression is "worse"? In various arenas, people more easily claim low-rank status than high-rank status. Even my executive coaching clients complain about their low rank and the seemingly insurmountable forces against which they have to contend.

Across the board, low rank is a stronger emotion than high rank. In fact, low rank is *limbic.*

The limbic system is the area of the brain in charge of managing emotion and forming memory. It's ground zero for our instinctual fears and motivations. Under threat, the limbic system—our emotional brain—kicks into gear. The amygdala sends signals that flood us with hormones, activating our response.

From an evolutionary standpoint, low rank is a matter of life and death: you're at the mercy of something or someone with greater power. You could be killed, hurt, or eaten. It's a classic fight, flight, or freeze moment. Even if we're not physically threatened, we still respond with the same surge of hormones. Our emotional brain doesn't parse probabilities. A curt email or a demeaning look can trigger the same reaction as a charging tiger.

"Wait!" You may argue. "High rank is emotional too. It feels great! I feel proud, confident, and assertive!" But didn't I just explain, in the last chapter, how stepping into a high-status role makes us feel more confident, disinhibited, and in control? High rank certainly has an emotional charge, but those emotions are not *life threatening* ones. The emotions associated with low rank—fear, hurt, outrage, depression, and anger—signal danger, and thus take priority over anything else happening in that moment, including the positive emotions of your high-ranking role.

Across many domains, psychologists have demonstrated what they refer to as the *negativity bias*: negative events, emotions, and memories take precedent over positive ones, every time.[2] Negative memories last longer than positive ones; there are more words for negative emotional states than there are for positive feelings; people fear negative feedback far more than they anticipate positive feedback; and so on. The emotional impact and psychological effects of bad experiences far outweigh that of happy ones. As Roy Baumeister, Professor of Psychology at Florida State University, co-author of an article titled "Bad Is Stronger Than Good,"[3] writes:

> [B]ad emotions, bad parents, and bad feedback have more impact than good ones, and bad information is processed more thoroughly than good. The self is more motivated to avoid bad self-definitions than to pursue good ones.[4]

Under stress, attack, or great pressure, the force of low rank clouds our ability to stay mindful of our high-ranking role. On April 20, 2010, when the Deepwater Horizon offshore drilling platform exploded, claiming eleven lives and spewing over two hundred million gallons of oil into the Gulf of Mexico, it caused massive environmental, economic, and social destruction. Speaking shortly after the event, Tony Hayward, then-CEO of British Petroleum—the company responsible for the tragedy—caused uproar when he said that while the event disrupted the lives of residents near the Gulf, it was also taking a toll on his personal life.

"I'd like my life back," he said, putting his discomfort on par with others, including those who had lost their lives or loved ones in the explosion.[5]

Hayward fell prey to the low-rank feelings right at the moment when he should have been most mindful of his high-ranking role. How could he have avoided this blunder? How can we stay mindful of high rank when the force of low rank is so great? Remember that motive is a *potential* factor—it's a catalyst. Whether we act on our feelings of low rank or not, whether that "amygdala hijack" takes over or not is up to us. Low rank is a motive, but not an all-powerful, inevitable one. It depends on our emotional self-management tools.

Robert Greene, author of *The 48 Laws of Power*, contends that managing your emotions is the prerequisite for successfully enacting the laws of power.[6] Before you can master power, you have to master your own emotional world.

Mastering Our Emotions
and the Secret of Self-Sourced Power

We all are bound by painful life experiences: getting bullied, being abandoned, growing up in poverty, or living in a dysfunctional alcoholic home—all can create enough of a sense of insecurity to overshadow the effects of other, high ranks. Traumatic experiences can drop our self-perceived power, but they can also elevate it: we can transform our pain into powerful life lessons, fortifying a foundation of resilience and strength that will carry us through whatever challenges life serves us.

Developing ourselves through and beyond our early emotional experiences is the work of our emotional self-management system, a complex set of skills and tools we each start developing in infancy. We learn to soothe ourselves when we feel anxious or fearful and to manage our hurt and anger when others treat us unfairly. The skills of emotional maturity begin in childhood, but take a lifetime to fully develop. Even when we've equipped ourselves with the tools to live with our difficult emotions, life continually sends us greater challenges: losing a loved one, becoming ill, getting fired, being left by someone we love, being the target of discrimination or harassment, going bankrupt, being sent to combat, or being humiliated in public by our boss.

Our ability to deal with emotions is inconsistent. Sometimes coping is easy. When it's not, if we can't do it ourselves, we turn to something or someone else to help us feel better. There are forms of healthy reliance: we talk to friends or counselors, take a walk, listen to music, meditate, or go to church. But there are also less healthy choices: taking drugs or alcohol to dampen the pain, or controlling, bullying, and manipulating the people and circumstances around us. When satisfying our needs depends on changing what's *outside* us rather than what's on the *inside*, we aren't managing ourselves— we are managing others.

High rank affords us an opportunity to satisfy personal needs by managing others instead of managing our emotions. Whenever you use your power to feel better about yourself, cover up insecurities, avoid a difficult conversation, or make life a little easier at someone else's expense, you've fixed a problem (briefly), but you've done so with the wrong set of tools.

High rank of any kind—be it position, strength of will, ability to gather allies and gossip about someone—can provide momentary relief or defense, but it comes at the cost of your development. If you hit someone who hurts your feelings, you might feel better temporarily, but you've become an aggressor and have done nothing to address why your self-worth depends on another's evaluation. If you gossip and spread rumors about someone who insulted you, you may feel a rush of satisfaction by getting revenge, but you've just diminished your reputation by identifying yourself as untrustworthy.

Power, like a substance, can be a shortcut to feeling better. If we feel weak, we can force compliance, gather allies, gossip, and form cliques. We can flatter people above us and bully those below. Or, like me in that 10th grade class, we can hide our deficiencies behind our role, and outwardly act competent and unruffled.

The motive to self-manage our emotions through our role is a temptation we face daily. Consider Charles, a recently divorced professor who, at the age of fifty-four, is afraid he'll never have another relationship. All day long he's surrounded by young, impressionable students. They admire his intelligence and, seeking his approval, act obsequious. What would stop him from crossing the line—from simply enjoying the attention, to encouraging it? What would stop you from assigning a few extra night shifts to someone on your team because he insulted you? Can you be certain the student who challenged you in class really deserves a C for her paper while the student who admires you deserves an A? Can you trust your objectivity, given your feelings?

With enough leeway, we grow dependent on shortcuts. Whenever we use something other than ourselves, something outside of ourselves, we have created a dependency, like with an addiction. Social power, by its nature, is outside of our control. Whether positional or by dint of our social identity, the rank we enjoy from our social role is defined and ratified by someone or something outside of ourselves: others' judgments, an organizational hierarchy, social norms and values, subordinates' compliance. If we rely on our social power for feelings of self-esteem, we lean on something we don't control, and, therefore, put ourselves in an unstable position. Like Gollum in *The Lord of the Rings*, we grow weak internally through our dependency. Without an inner source of self-esteem, we become ever more dependent and desperate to maintain equilibrium.

We sense when someone's self-esteem depends on their social role. We get embroiled in propping up another's status. I felt this often with teachers. My 9th grade history teacher, Mr. Westwood, was renowned for his obsession with seating posture. We had to face front, feet on the floor, hands on our desk, books open. He made us read from our textbook, silently, for forty minutes every day. He was without a doubt the worst teacher I ever had. He spent the entire class focusing on managing our postures, and none of it teaching history.

Mrs. Baldini, my 11th grade political science teacher, was also renowned—but for another reason: her incredibly high standards. Unlike other teachers, she didn't spend time managing classroom dynamics. She didn't have to. No one ever, ever dared act up in her classroom.

Mr. Westwood taught from his position; Mrs. Baldini taught from her passion. They both had positional power. They both had authority. But Mr. Westwood's sense of authority depended on our discipline and compliance. Mrs. Baldini's authority, on the other hand, came from her knowledge and enthusiasm for the topic. When she entered the room, we could sense her authority was independent of our behavior. She knew her subject matter, and it didn't matter whether we thought so. With Mr. Westwood, we felt tangled up in his legitimacy. *He needed our behavior to ratify his authority.* His "teacherness" depended on what we did, not on what he felt about himself.

Just as energy derives from many sources (oil, solar, hydro, natural gas, nuclear, coal) so does human power. Power has many sources. Some sources are personal and internal, while others are social and external. Social power extracts its validity from other people. It's outsourced power. It only becomes real and valid when others legitimize it. And, just like energy, external or foreign sources create *entanglements*, messy and complicated relationships and dependencies on others, destabilizing over time.

While social power is based in the external, personal power is self-sourced. Its greatest value is that it doesn't depend on others for validity. Mrs. Baldini had personal power, because she relied on her knowledge, personality, life experience, ability to get along with people, and social skills. Personal power exists independently of others' endorsement.

All this leads back to motive. The motive for misusing high rank starts with having poor emotional self-management tools. You rely on outsourced, not in-sourced power. You use your social power, and not personal power, to soothe, protect, and defend yourself. Your sense of self hinges on what the other does or doesn't do. You gain your rank through external compliance or validation. You have motive to use your role for personal gain.

Personal power is the immunity from motive. It's an immunity we need. It's the rudder, the guiding compass in how well we use our power. The only power that can transfer from context to context, that can withstand the limbic threat of low rank, that isn't subject to emotional turmoil, is in-sourced power, that which comes from within: our personal power.

Yes, the solution to powerlessness is more power—more *personal* power, that is.

The Power You Can Take With You: Personal Power

He's almost become a cliché, but one of the best examples of personal power in our time is Nelson Mandela.

Mandela spent twenty-seven years as a political prisoner during South Africa's apartheid regime, living in an eight-by-seven-foot cement cell furnished only with a straw mat. White prison wardens verbally berated and physically abused him. Because he had been sentenced to prison indefinitely, he was stripped of all human rights. He wasn't just on the lower rungs of authority; he wasn't even on the ladder. And yet he saw himself as a teacher and moral guide—to other prisoners, to guards, and to the government. He said he saw his trial as an opportunity to teach.[7]

Mandela *felt* powerful. He considered himself a leader, even though no one else ratified it. He had no social status, no resources, nothing but his own deep well of insight and wisdom. What he had was personal power. It was sourced in himself, and it did not depend on anyone else for its value.

Personal power is an inner feeling of power that reverberates regardless of what happens to us. Mindell describes in great detail the value and the source of personal power, especially when it comes to negotiating conflict.[8] In his framework of rank, personal power is a combination of psychological abilities, life experiences, emotional intelligence, and spiritual strength.

Consider the story of Viktor Frankl, who spent three years in a concentration camp and lost his wife, parents, and brother to the Nazis. His insight from that experience became the foundation of humanistic psychotherapy: human freedom is the freedom to choose our attitude in any given circumstance.[9] All of our freedoms may be taken away, save one: the freedom to choose to respond to what happens to us. When we cannot change a situation, Frankl says, "we are challenged to change ourselves."[10] This is personal power: the ability to change ourselves and to get along with even impossible situations.

Personal power is the power within us to achieve success, be effective at what we do, and make our world a better place. Personal power is the sum total of the unique personality traits, abilities, talents, and experience each of us brings to the table. Personal power —and not social power—is what you reach for when your loved one dies. You draw upon personal power when you have to have a difficult conversation. Personal power comforts you when you are diagnosed with a terrifying illness or when you lose your job and find yourself homeless and alone. Personal power helps you roll with whatever life throws at you, to stay afloat as the waves come crashing in.

It's what leaders reach for when they stand in front of a skeptical or hostile crowd. It's what you need to make people feel motivated and engaged. It's what you use to cultivate nourishing relationships with your family, friends, and community. Personal power is the secret sauce, the special ingredient that makes you succeed, whether you're a senator, secretary, or car salesman.

If you're a meditator, you might call personal power *mindfulness*, because it includes your ability to be aware yet detached and non-reactive.

If you're a psychologist, you might call it *positive self-regard*, because personal power is a sense of self-esteem independent of others' perceptions.

If you're a military or political leader, you might think of personal power as *character*, because it means being honest with yourself and having the integrity to stand for what you believe in.

If you're a follower of religion or a spiritual person, you might see personal power as *loving kindness*, because it doesn't ask you to coerce, demand from, or manipulate others.

If you're in business, personal power comprises your ability to *influence* others to meet your objectives.

If you're a student of political science, you might call personal power *moral authority* or *soft power*: the power to create alliances and support, and to have people follow you out of choice—not out of force.

Personal power is available to everyone, regardless of education, age, class, wealth, size, race, and gender. It never needs to be validated by others. You—not your society, organization, or community—*you* determine your degree of personal power.

Positional power needs the counterbalance that personal power brings. It's what we use to be effective in our positional roles. On one hand, without personal power we can overly rely on our positions, becoming bureaucratic or authoritarian. On the other hand, without personal power, we fail to step fully into our positional power and do what the task requires of us.[11]

In many ways, personal power accounts for how well or poorly we use our authority overall. High positional authority and low personal power beget illegitimate leadership. On the flipside, in instances when we lack positional power, high personal power allows us to accomplish amazing things because of our ability to influence others. Figure 2.1 below shows the different ways we tend to use our authority with different levels of positional and personal power.

So how do we develop our personal power? In a sense, we don't —not entirely, or not always consciously. Personal power is innate and developed, both born and made. We derive personal power from our personality, build it through life experience, and cultivate it through the hard work of self-development. Like the Lion, Scarecrow, and Tin Man in *The Wizard of Oz*, we *already* possess the solution we seek but often don't know it. Sometimes our personal powers lie underdeveloped or are misdirected. Culture teaches us to value certain traits and attributes, and so we minimize or even criticize those aspects of our own personalities that don't fit those standards. But our personality is the soil out of which our personal power blossoms. Cultivating personal power starts with knowing and valuing who you are.

This is nowhere near as easy as it sounds. Each of us is unique. There's no fan club at the ready to make us feel secure about our individuality. Being yourself is a lonely road. It takes courage. No one else brings the exact talents, perspectives, and approaches you do. And so, while the contribution you make is of the utmost importance, you may find it extremely hard to stand for.

The best chance we have to manage our emotional motives is by growing our personal power, our greatest asset for good and strongest weapon against the corrupting influence of power. The next chapters will introduce you to your "Powerprint" and guide you through creating an inventory of all your powers. What different sorts of powers do you have, and where do they come from? What influences from childhood continue to echo today, impacting your use of power? What are your weaknesses and assets? The following chapter and subsequent Powerprint exercise will answer these questions, guiding you in how to develop the raw material of your personality and life experiences into a robust personal power—a superpower you can transfer across all contexts.

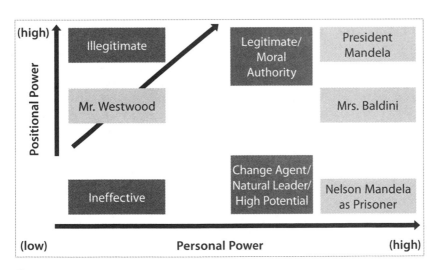

Figure 2.1

GETTING STARTED:
FIND YOUR POWERPRINT

࿊

The influence you exert is through your own life,
and what you've become yourself.

—ELEANOR ROOSEVELT

3

Powerprints:
Your Unique Picture of Power

A man's true state of power and riches is to be in himself.

—HENRY WARD BEECHER

T hough people often describe it with metaphors like ladders and pyramids, power is not quite a hierarchy. Actually, it's more like a complex web. If you read the preceding chapter, you will be familiar with two kinds of power, which you can think of as sides of a holistic, capital-P "Power": there's social power, outsourced and dependent on external values, such as your positional power, or your social status; and there's personal power, the innermost strength found in the essence of who you are, and forged in the fires of life experience. Indeed, the power a person has emerges out of the confluence of many different factors. Like weather, which can't be predicted by one variable alone, power is a dynamic interaction between the role you play and your social identity, history, personality, state of mind, emotions, and momentary cultural context.

Power is more like a complex system than a hierarchy of positions. And in this complex system, there is no hierarchy, no ranking of ranks

—just a collection of different ranks, social and personal, based on various factors: assets and life experiences, social status and position, physical and mental health, birth order, family and community attachment. In this interconnected web of power, intangible powers are just as important as tangible ones. The social is just as meaningful as the personal. Think of power's complex system as you would a fingerprint. Except in this case, it's your *Powerprint*: an intricate pattern of interconnected, overlapping, and sometimes contradictory capabilities and strengths. Like fingerprints, no two Powerprints are alike. Each is its own unique mix of life experiences, traits, and social statuses, as well as physical, psychological, and social abilities. Let's explore the concept of Powerprints further through the stories of Dan, Claudia, and Tahir, three people born on the same day in 1972.[1]

Dan grew up in a wealthy family. He attended private schools and eventually the same Ivy League college as his father and grandfather before him. These days, Dan earns a very good living working for a major corporation. He is white, male, Protestant, and heterosexual. He can trace his lineage all the way back to the American Revolution. Without a doubt, Dan won the social status lottery.

While Dan was growing up in Ohio, Claudia was growing up in a poor neighborhood outside San Antonio, Texas. Claudia's father had to return to Mexico before she was born, and her mother died when she was five. After that, she and her two younger sisters went to live with their aunt and uncle. Despite her early losses, Claudia did well in school. She was popular with the other children and with her teachers. But shortly after she turned sixteen, Claudia had to drop out: her uncle suffered an accident at the factory, and someone needed to help support the family.

Meanwhile, halfway across the world, Tahir was growing up in a small village outside of Manchester, UK. His family emigrated from Pakistan when he was eight. As one of only two non-white children in his entire school, Tahir had to put up with bullying and harassment. Every day, kids followed him home from school, throwing stones and calling him a "Paki."

If we talk about power the conventional way, the way we're used to, it's pretty easy to say who has more and who has less power, right?

But there's more—a lot more—to each story.

Since early childhood, Dan suffered from severe asthma. In elementary school, he spent weeks in bed, isolated from other children. He wasn't allowed to play sports because of his condition. His protective and concerned parents monitored all of his comings and goings. Still, he was lucky to have been born into a family with the means to care for his condition. Poorer children, lacking access to the level of healthcare Dan possessed, may not have survived.

But Dan felt neither lucky nor privileged. Because he couldn't play sports, and was often absent from school, he was unpopular and socially awkward. Other kids teased him for being skinny and weak. He often felt fearful, weak, and lonely. His high social status did nothing for him in this regard. Today, he still carries with him a sense of insecurity. His early health scares left him with anxiety and an acute fear of death. When faced with stress, his anxiety worsens; he panics he won't be able to cope with challenges. This liability shows up in his professional life. At work, he tends to be indecisive, standoffish, and pessimistic. Because of his social insecurity, he has trouble connecting to others and has few close friends. While others around him rise higher in the organization, Dan's career trajectory has stalled thanks to his issues. Despite his very high social status, Dan's dominant inner experience of himself is that of weakness.

Though Claudia lost her mother and never knew her father, she lived with a doting aunt and uncle, and was surrounded by an extended family: every weekend, other aunts and uncles, cousins, and close family friends would gather together. Her warm and loving family made her feel cared for and safe. Claudia grew up in poverty, as an immigrant, without parents, without completing high school. She's on the "lowest rungs of the ladder." Had she suffered from Dan's health problems, with her low socio-economic status, she might not have survived.

Emotionally, however, Claudia thrives. She's confident in her ability to make friends and get by in the world. She isn't intimidated by challenges and has a strong sense of identity and purpose. Claudia always knew one day she would go back to school and become a nurse. In fact, that's what she did at the age of twenty-five. Now in her forties, she's an instructor at a nursing school as well as an important mentor to students and junior colleagues.

Tahir grew up scared and lonely, but his classmates' taunts only made him more determined to succeed. Secretly, he felt superior to them. His family was more educated: his father was a mathematics professor at the local university, and his mother was a doctor. At home, he was supported and encouraged. His sense of intelligence was reinforced by his performance: he did better in school than the other kids. Tahir always knew he would be more successful than his adversaries in life due to his intelligence and access to education. At eleven years old, with an awareness of other cultures and countries, he already felt worldly.

Dan, Claudia, and Tahir have diametrically different personal experiences of power. Their narratives are not unique; each of us has a similar story. Their life stories, as do ours, demonstrate how complex power truly is. It is a system composed from many different influences including society, family, physical health, intelligence, personality, lineage, school, friends, and more.

Dan had social power based on status and demographics such as race, gender, and social class. Tahir derived power from his intelligence, his social class, cultural vantage point and his family's support for his education. Claudia drew upon a different kind of power altogether—the power of personality, family support, cultural heritage, and a sense of belonging.

Social activists and academics refer to the myriad social identities we possess as "intersectionality": overlapping and interconnected social categories. But while intersectionality focuses on different *external* categories, a Powerprint also takes into account what lies beneath: our subjective, perceived sense of power.

As you start to think about what your own Powerprint looks like, consider several important characteristics of power Claudia, Tahir, and Dan's stories teach us:

What You See Is Not What You Get

As you move through the world, those around you perceive and pass judgment about the disadvantages and advantages you have—your objective powers. Some of these qualities relate to your social identity: skin color, gender, age, and nationality. Others have to do with less tangible characteristics such as intelligence, confidence, and social skills.

No matter what your objective powers seem to be, what people see is not necessarily what you *feel*. What you feel is your *self-perceived power*, which does not always correspond with what the world sees in you. Others can only perceive the visible things about us like our skin color and gender, as well as how we dress, move, and speak. From there, people project their stereotypes, judgments, and expectations onto us. Sure, how we appear is a big part of our power identity, but as with Dan, Claudia, and Tahir, it's not the whole story.

Self-Perceived Power
Significantly Determines Our Sense of Well-Being

The world can define our social status, and it's important to be aware of the privileges and challenges resulting from that definition, but how we survive and get by in life on a moment-to-moment basis depends as much—if not more—on our self-perceived power. Claudia and Tahir felt powerful, even though they were subjected to racism and bullying. They suffered social discrimination and no doubt, to some degree, internalized their oppression. Yet the discrimination they suffered did not fully define their self-image and sense of self-esteem.

Similarly, Dan's feelings were also impervious to his social status, but in the opposite direction. His privilege and high social position did not help him feel powerful. Those qualities couldn't penetrate his feelings of fear and weakness, nor his isolation from his community. His frail health produced a lingering sense of low power that shaped his self-image, despite the high social status of his circumstances.

We Cannot Predict What Determines
Our Self-Perceived Power

Some experiences allow us to feel powerful, and others make us feel powerless. Health can bestow a sense of strength—or weakness. Tahir's intelligence trumped his experience of being bullied, but we can't trace how or why. Another kid in his position may have responded differently. He could have just as easily been ashamed of his family's education, feeling it set him apart further from his peer group.

When it comes to determining which experiences lend us resilience and which hamper us, people are individuals. Some, for instance, feel their birth order matters; others' feelings of power, high or low, are connected to their sense of intelligence. Our power landscape is a convoluted equation, in which the sum of different variables of rank and identity cannot predict how powerful we ultimately feel.

We each are unique in this way. There's no one scale or chart we can point to in order to predict what will make us feel powerful and what will drop our sense of authority. What I do see in my work with clients, however, is childhood experiences often play a part.

Our Historical Views of Power Play a Major Part in Our Use of Power as Adults

Childhood, it seems, lasts forever. Our experiences as children are extremely predictive of and decisive in our later lives. Perhaps because our brains are still developing, our earliest experiences have a profound influence on our personality and development. What we learn in childhood can become a pattern that can stay with us our whole life. Perhaps we also skew the importance and weight of what happens to us earlier in our lifespans, because as children we have less control over what happens to us—less ability to make sense of its tribulations, and thus we spend a lifetime trying to make meaning from them. For these reasons, psychologically, we magnify the importance of our childhoods.

Our social status changes as we age, through education, growth, employment, and the like, but we never outgrow the power identity we grew up with. We don't enter positions of authority with a blank slate. Claudia's relationship with her family, Tahir's intellectual detachment from his bullies, and Dan's alienation due to his health issues—each occurrence shaped the way that person grew up. Like adults who were overweight as children, and still "feel fat" even if they are now normal-sized, we carry with us the vestiges of early rank experiences.

If you were the subject of discrimination, you no doubt internalized negative messages about your identity. If you were constantly compared to an older sister or brother whom all your teachers loved and who got A-pluses in every subject, you can still feel foolish in spite of your advanced degree. If you were bullied because you wore glasses or the wrong clothes, if you grew up in an alcoholic family, suffered abuse, or had serious health issues as a child, like Dan, your insecurity can still haunt you today, even if you occupy an important position and take home a six-figure income.

Childhood experiences also echo in the other, positive direction. If you felt loved and embraced, supported and encouraged, you can feel a sense of high internal rank in the face of discrimination, financial hardship, or have health problems that make you less able and fit than others. The emotional support we received as children can buoy us through the roughest waters.

What We Feel May Not Be Real

At the end of the day, how well we use our power, and to what extent, is determined by the person we're trying to influence. We gauge our influence by how the other experiences it. If Tahir's abuse doesn't faze him, his bullies have no power over him. We may feel or believe in our authority, but whether we make an impact with it or not, depends on others' perceptions.

We need to be cognizant of how we "land"—the impression that our words, behavior, nonverbal signals, and feelings leave on others. Others often pre-judge us based on their perception of our objective powers and social identity markers like gender, skin color, size, accent, et cetera. Sometimes we have positional authority, and high social status, but like Dan, our ability to make a positive influence lags.

Our task is to be able to close the gap between what others see, what we feel, and the impact we make. The power of emotions is such that it's easy to believe that what we feel—our self-perceived rank—is *real*, that is, others experience it. This is the tricky thing about behavior, feelings, and power: like Luis, we feel under threat, but that's not what others perceive. On the other hand, we can be dealt a difficult hand, but feel good about ourselves, which in turn influences how others experience us.

As we grapple with our feelings of rank, low and high, we need to stay mindful of the reality that the impact we make on the people we interact with may not be the same as what we feel.

These five points describe the "inner workings" of power, forming the foundation of how we understand and, eventually, wield our power with purpose and awareness. We are now at the end of the theoretical chapters of the *User's Guide* and are approaching the book's practical component. Before we move ahead, let's recap and sum up what we know so far about power—what makes it corrupting, what makes us corruptible, and the inner workings that drive our power use:

1) **High rank has psychological effects that alter our behavior and attitude, the means of power.** Power corrupts absolutely, but not inevitably.

2) **High rank comes bundled with opportunity for its misuse.** When we occupy a position of power, people act differently around us, we receive less feedback, our behavior is subject to the self-fulfilling prophecies of others, and our rank protects us from influences outside the role.

3) **Motive determines how we use power.** A main motive for misusing power is feeling weak. We use our rank to manage emotions, feel better about ourselves, protect and defend ourselves.

4) **The way we use power depends on our self-perceived power.** Alongside our multiple, objective powers are our self-perceived feelings of power. Since how we feel largely dictates our behavior, our self-perceived power plays a big part in how we use power. If our self-perceived rank is low, we can be tempted to use our social rank in self-serving ways.

5) **Context plays a role in defining power.** Each context has a different set of values, which determines what behavior, resources, and abilities have power, and which influences our *feelings* of power, our self-perceived power, and hence how well or poorly we use it.

6) **Social power is "outsourced," dependent upon external values, norms, and hierarchies.** Its greatest liability is that it doesn't transfer from context to context. Relying on social power—whether in our position or our social status—to feel powerful creates dependencies. It entangles our self-esteem with others' behavior and judgments.

7) **Personal power, unlike social power, is "self-sourced."** It comes from within, and is therefore more stable and robust. Personal power is the power "you can take with you." It transfers from context to context.

8) **We each have a Powerprint,** a unique, complex system of overlapping, intersecting, and—at times—contradictory rank experiences, which includes social and personal, tangible and intangible power.

We can now update our definition of power, as well as what it means to use power well. In the Introduction, I defined power as the ability to impact and influence our environment. Putting that together with what we've learned about a) the role of self-perceived power and the motive of feeling weak; b) the role of context in determining how powerful we feel; c) the frailty of outsourced (social) power; and finally, d) the robustness of insourced (personal) power; our updated definition is this:

Power, when used responsibly and effectively, is the ability to impact and influence situations across diverse and unpredictable contexts with legitimacy (implied or explicit cooperation and agreement of others) for the greater good.

The next chapter, Chapter 4, is an exercise you can use to discover your Powerprint. This exercise gives you an opportunity to look at your objective powers (including your social, personal, and historical power), and also get to know your self-perceived power, the power you feel, which underlies how you influence others.

The Powerprint will allow you to see your different power assets and also your liabilities: places where you lack power or the feeling of power. Most important, this exercise will equip you to make the best use of the subsequent guidelines for power. You will know with precision how well you already use your power, and where and how you can improve.

4

Find Your Powerprint

Character is power.

—BOOKER T. WASHINGTON

his chapter introduces a learning activity, and requires nothing more than time and your own self-reflection. You will be guided through a series of questions (in the Appendix) to help you create your Powerprint, an inventory of your power: your social and personal powers, your historical power, and the influences from childhood that impact your use of power today. The exercise helps you discover your greatest assets, as well as your liabilities that could act as motive to misuse power. Getting to know your Powerprint will help you understand which of the coming guidelines on power are most useful to you in the chapters following in Section III.

Before you embark on this activity, I recommend you write down the most pressing question or questions you have about power.

- Are you worried about the pressures of your leadership role?
- Do you want to feel more empowered and grounded in your authority with friends, family, or colleagues?

- Are you interested in using power to make change, to challenge existing power structures?
- Have you received feedback that you enact your power too timidly or too harshly, or erratically?

The Powerprint exercise won't directly address specific problems, but the insights and awareness you gain about your power will shed light on your concerns.

Give yourself at least an hour, preferably two, to work through this exercise. You can read through it now and come back to it when you have more time. The exercise itself won't take very long, but the questions in it may provoke some deep thinking that warrants more time for reflection.

Whenever you do it, make sure you find a quiet place where you won't be easily interrupted. Turn off your phone, close the door, and do what you can to make an untroubled and private space for yourself. Be sure to keep a journal or other writing surface nearby to jot down your thoughts and reflections. If you prefer, you can do this activity online at https://diamondleadership.com/leadership-resources/powerprint-worksheet/.

Before You Begin...

1) ***There are no right answers.*** This is self-discovery, not math. There are no right and wrong answers, nor is there just one answer. This exercise is designed for you to learn about your world of power. As you read through the questions, you are likely to have many different answers and responses, even conflicting ones! You could—and should—have complex answers. Remember, a Powerprint is unique and individual: there is no norm, no percentile to benchmark your answers. Your Powerprint reflects you and you alone. In fact, you can do this exercise several times; each time, you may see another facet of your story, and become aware of different strengths and opportunities.

2) **You may feel uncomfortable.** You will be asked questions about your life experiences at present day and in the past. These questions may bring up unpleasant memories and feelings. Go forward only if you feel able to be with what may surface. If you do find yourself having difficult feelings, you can work on it with a friend, coach, therapist, or someone who could help you sort through the feelings you have. And feel free to skip the question if it's too difficult, or skip the exercise altogether, and come back at a time when you feel able to sit with what comes up. You may see things in a new light, which could be enlightening and informative, but also provocative and challenging. This is an educational experience, and all learning has a little bit of discomfort to it, as new information jostles what we have previously believed to be true. Keep an open—and skeptical—mindset.

3) **It's important to describe your objective social identity as well your personal experience of it.** Some readers may be well-versed in the dynamics of power and rank, and familiar with diversity and inclusion work. Though these questions concern your social identity, power, and privileges, they also seek to uncover your personal, subjective, and utterly unique experiences of those attributes. A Powerprint is not just a social analysis; it is a deeply subjective, complex, and personal one. Remember the stories of Dan, Claudia, and Tahir? *Consider both the objective facts of your social identity, and your subjective, personal experience of it.*

4) **The higher your social rank, the less you may notice it.** The very definition of high social rank is that it's something you don't have to worry about. High social rank means having social or psychological advantages, which result in comfort and a sense of belonging and entitlement. If you

were born wealthy, financial stress might not be something you think about much. If, as a kid, you were fairly athletic and coordinated, you didn't have anxiety about being left out or chosen last on the football teams. If you got good grades in school, when it comes to speaking about theories, you might not sweat too much. If you are heterosexual, you grew up surrounded by examples of relationships in which you saw yourself. Talking about dating and sex may feel normal to you. As you read through these questions, if you find yourself thinking, "Hmm, this isn't important to me," "I never thought about it," or, "I don't see color, gender, or class difference," then entertain the possibility that you might have higher rank than others.

5) ***There are highs and lows to both high and low rank.*** I can't repeat it enough: your personal, subjective experience of power is complex. High rank bestows privileges, but can also be a source of difficulty and even incapacity. Some high-rank experiences have shielded you from experiences and challenges, which now result in a lack of emotional or social skills. Low social rank came with enormous suffering, but you may also notice social skills, inner wisdom, or self-esteem that grew out of the ability to surmount those challenges.

As you read through the list below, you will be asked to consider **both** the **strengths** and **challenges** each experience brought. Strengths may include social advantages and privileges, such as money or education, but they also may include emotional and social skills, or skills and abilities you've gained or grown such as self-awareness and resilience. And things change over time. You may have suffered more when you were younger, and are now in touch with the strengths you gained. Or perhaps you had an easier time when you were young, but now realize some of what you missed. All of this is important. Try to identify everything that arises and remain honest with yourself.

There are two sections to the exercise:

1) Take an Inventory of Your Powers
2) Tell the Story of Your Powerprint

Ready to go? Get your paper and pen and flip to page 201, or go online and find this exercise at https://diamondleadership.com/leadership-resources/powerprint-worksheet/.

SECTION III

THE GUIDELINES FOR POWER

*When you are content to be simply yourself and don't compare
or compete, everyone will respect you.*

—LAO TZU

First, Cultivate Your Traits

Success is liking yourself, liking what you do,
and liking how you do it.

—MAYA ANGELOU

Care about people's approval
and you will be their prisoner.

—LAO TZU

You lead as you live. When you step into a position of power —leader, teacher, therapist, pastor, parent—you don't change personalities. You are who you've always been. There are millions of books and blogs out there that will tell you the traits, habits, and skills you need to be a successful leader. You can learn new behaviors, develop skills, and tame those aspects of your personality that derail you, but you cannot develop a personality you don't already have. You're pretty much stuck with yourself.

If you like yourself, that's a good thing. If you don't, and you're in a position of power, it might be time to start.

Liking yourself may not come naturally, or easily. Indeed, you may be reading this and thinking, "I don't like myself." If so, don't make that another reason to not like yourself! Many people take a lifetime to find inner support and learn to treat themselves with dignity. It's never too late to start, and just a little bit of self-love goes a long way. If this speaks to you, and you haven't filled out the

Powerprint exercise, I suggest you flip ahead to the Appendix and return here after thoroughly completing the exercise.

If you're akin to most people, you appreciate certain parts of yourself, and other parts less so. But playing favorites with your personality puts you at a disadvantage. Your personality is the raw material from which your personal power grows. And growing your personal power starts with developing that raw material—cultivating your traits. Your first task is to get to know, like, and learn how to use the personality you have—all of it.

The word "cultivate" comes from the Medieval Latin *cultivatus*, meaning "to till or farm." Like a garden, a personality needs to be tended. It must be watered, fed, and pruned to grow in the way that's useful for our needs. A trait can be an asset or liability—it depends on how you cultivate it. Cultivation entails adding awareness and self-reflection, as well as learning how and where to direct our natures, and how to temper them.

For instance, the trait of self-assuredness, without awareness, can develop into closed-mindedness: being averse to learning new things. An easygoing and relaxed personality trait can, lacking direction, transform into laziness and apathy, allowing us to miss opportunities that require effort, or leaving us unable to follow through with difficult tasks. One can harness assertiveness for leadership, or it can grow, like a weed, into overbearing and bossy behavior.

Whatever we don't cultivate or direct in a useful manner becomes a liability—a power "leak," a place where we lose effectiveness. My innate drive helps me accomplish my goals but also makes me tense and irritable. My capacity to get things going is a terrific asset; the flip side, my impatience, is a major power drain.

As trite as it might sound, the first step in cultivating your traits is to know yourself and like yourself. *What makes a trait a source of power is our comfort with it.* No one trait is better than another; no one trait is more powerful than another. If we are comfortable in our introversion, others will be too. If we come to appreciate our bossiness, and see it as potential leadership, it will aid us as a great ally. The idea is to take a supposedly negative tendency (such as conflict avoidance) and turn it into an advantage (diplomacy, "people skills"). There are great things in every trait, just as there are drawbacks associated with each. Every trait is a double-edged sword. We only have to learn how to wield that sword.

The rules of growing your personal power start with these guidelines for cultivating your traits:

Guideline #1: Let Your Freak Flag Fly

Imagine this: A poor, uneducated man decides to run for president. He comes from an isolated, rural community where he never finished grade school, let alone went to college. He speaks grammatically incorrect English in a thick, country drawl, peppered with slang. He's gangly and awkward. His clothes don't fit him properly. What's more, he suffers terrible mood swings, fluctuating between happiness and a despondent depression. When cheerful, he's gregarious and charming, but he also veers into socially inappropriate territory, telling long, rambling stories, and dirty, politically incorrect jokes.

Hard to imagine someone like him running for president. Not only did this man run for office, but he also got elected. Twice. You know him. He's Abraham Lincoln, thought today to be one of the greatest—if not the greatest—American presidents.

Lincoln's unique personality is the subject of thousands of books. He may be the most written about figure in American history. It's not just our modern sensibilities that make Lincoln appear unique. He was odd by the standards of his day. His peculiar and unsophisticated mannerisms provided plenty of fodder for his opponents, who mimicked and mocked him, calling him a buffoon, barbarian, clown, and gorilla—the latter of which cartoonists frequently used to portray him.

The remarkable thing about Lincoln was that he didn't try to fit in. We don't know if, and to what degree, he minded the mockery. What we do know is that he never adjusted his style. He never adopted different mannerisms. In fact, he probably wouldn't have succeeded had he tried.

Instead, Lincoln cultivated his traits. He used his folksy, down-home personality to his advantage. He didn't hide his backwoods nature. He didn't hire a speech coach to modify his Kentucky accent, or a fashion consultant to find him better-tailored suits. He didn't do anything to act the part of president, but everything to act the part of himself.

Lincoln knew who he was and who he wasn't. He appreciated and cultivated his traits, and used them as powers: the power to connect with people, to communicate across divides, to engage with his opponents, and to gain the trust of the nation. His phenomenal ability to relate to people across vast political schisms and find the common humanity beneath was his great, self-sourced power. It was a power he employed as a critical asset during his tenure—a period of unparalleled social and economic upheaval, not to mention the deadliest time in the history of the United States.

Task number one in cultivating your traits is coming to terms with who you are, on a sincere level. What hand were you dealt? You will find tremendous comfort and, ultimately, power, by knowing who you are. Whenever you try to fit in or hide things about yourself, acting out the persona you think others want to see, you become vulnerable to criticism. You become dependent on others' perceptions when you try to live up to their expectations. You put your self-esteem into others' hands, letting your barometer of self-worth rise and fall with their opinions.

But when you have nothing to lose—when you embrace your quirks and use them—you become unassailable. People can criticize you, but your best defense is to know and love yourself, especially your foibles. The better we are at appreciating the hand we're dealt, our special personality with all its eccentricities and foibles, the easier it is to utilize it as a power.

It doesn't matter how we find or define our traits; what's important is that we appreciate them all and learn to use them to our advantage. This is no simple task. We have internalized a ranking system of personality traits. Growing up is a process of socialization, of adapting to the norms of family and culture. It's in the nature of culture to prize certain behaviors over others as a means to socialize its members to adapt and survive. In cultures where famines frequently occurred, sharing and generosity are prized as a virtue, and stinginess eschewed. Some cultures and families uphold introversion, whereas others see it as anti-social behavior. At a workshop I facilitated in Greece, some participants confided to me that they didn't like socializing as much as their friends did, and felt not only guilty, but also that something perhaps was wrong with them. Due to this socialization process, most of us come out of childhood with two sets of traits: those we think are valuable, and those we feel make us "wrong" or "bad."

I once coached a senior product director for a major software company. He initially came for help to deal with his boss. After a few sessions, he told me he was afraid he didn't have what it took to succeed in that company. He wasn't as sharp, assertive, and competitive as the others. His style just didn't fit in, he said.

I asked him, "Well, what is your style?"

He thought for a moment and said, "I'm not competitive."

"Actually," he continued, "I think I'm more creative. I like designing new things, coming up with new ideas. But that's not part of my job now and that won't help me succeed."

We explored for a few minutes what he meant by "creative," and it came to light that his father was an artist, but not a financially successful one. In fact, the client's childhood was marked by frequent moves, financial hardships, and a lot of uncertainty due to his father's difficulty making a living. For my client, being "creative" was associated with failure, and yet creativity was his strong suit. After working together for a few months, he decided to find a better fit for his skills, and soon thereafter found a position at an apparel company. For the first time in his career, he enjoyed the feeling that his skills and style were appreciated and valued.

It is precisely these traits, the ones we fear are "bad" or "wrong" that we need to embrace. They are our "freak flags," our unique qualities, and great sources of strength—if we can get to know and cultivate them.

Think about superheroes. Their origins are the ultimate stories of peculiarities becoming great power. Superman was orphaned after an explosion killed his parents and destroyed his home planet. Spiderman was bitten by a radioactive spider. Batman watched his parents murdered in a mugging gone wrong. The Flash was struck by lightning. The Hulk was bathed in gamma radiation due to a faulty bomb detonation. All have, at one point or another, tried to hide their true identity, but learned to embrace their superheroic qualities—the traits they're afraid of—to save another's life. We love superhero myths because of this paradoxical mix of freakishness and heroism. Almost all of them are misfits, aliens, and outcasts. But the very thing that makes each an outsider is also the source of their superpower.

We are all superheroes; we are all a bit freakish in our own way. And to cultivate our traits, we have to fight the cultural programming that makes us try to fit in and be "cool." When we embrace our total self—the parts we like, and the ones we've been conditioned not to—then we have nothing to hide. Our inner freedom is the foundation for our personal power.

Doable Practice #1: Let Your Freak Flag Fly

Take a trait you don't like in yourself, or think doesn't serve you well, and find the positive in it. Try to reframe it, by asking yourself: How could this be an asset? Where could I use it in my life, and in my work? Where might I *already* be using it to my own and others' advantage?

Guideline #2: Tame Your Triggers

Loving yourself and embracing all your traits is a first step. Yet even when you love yourself, you have another vulnerability to watch out for: your emotional volatility. Certain things provoke us, and set off an emotional, limbic response before we know it. We call these things triggers. They are stimuli—sight, sounds, words, images—that remind us of earlier, traumatic or challenging events.

If we get triggered, reactive, or provoked, we can fall swiftly into a low-rank state. It is a drop in rank to be at the mercy of our feelings, other people, or the events around us. Remember Luis? He would get triggered by the topic of immigration and lose touch with his sense of power. Being triggered can look like a dramatic outburst, but it can also be subtle. Hovering parents are reacting to perceived dangers and threats. Though they don't appear overly emotional, they are overdoing it because they've been triggered by the fear that something bad may happen to their child.

A micro-managing boss might be reacting to triggers as well. I once coached a CEO whose response to anxiety was to walk around and peek his head into others' offices and sit in on meetings. His behavior annoyed everyone. He would add his two cents in situations and places where he had no idea what had already been discussed or what the issues were. Why? It made him feel like he was doing something, anything. He was attempting to combat his fears and his worry about the company's standing.

The greatest threat to building and maintaining our personal power is getting triggered. When we wield power from a triggered state of mind, we do so poorly: We react, rather than respond; attempt to control, rather than engage; and self-protect, instead of serving the whole. Handing power over to our reactions leaves us with the motive to misuse our power.

We can't do away with triggers, but we can learn about and control them. I will always be somewhat impatient. Luis, the professor who got fired, will always have a knee-jerk reaction in response to issues of immigration and social justice. The CEO will always be prone to anxiety. But knowing our triggers and being able to anticipate them gives us more control over them and more choice in how to respond. Taming triggers is the task of a lifetime. However, there are some things you can learn and practice:

Know your "wood to burn." We all have places where we've been hurt. These are the sources of our triggers, the "wood we have to burn." Arnold Mindell has spent thousands of hours working with groups in conflict, and coined the phrase, "wood to burn," the things that fuel our anger and upset.[1] "Wood" is all the issues we carry, the baggage that needs processing, the old wounds that need resolution. Burning your wood means working on these issues, understanding them, being mindful of the things that knock you off balance, and managing the emotions and reactions that follow. Some issues are long standing and have roots not only in personal history, but also in collective history: matters such as racism, sexism, homophobia, abuse, and trauma. Coming to terms with the issues that affect us is not a one-off activity but a life-long journey.

One of the most effective steps we can take is preparation. Know what is likely to sink you. Know what tends to trigger a low-rank response. Know your "wood piles" that need to be worked on, and know where and when they tend to surface. The best defense is a good offense. In this case, it means anticipating what words and behaviors are likely to trigger you, so you're not caught off guard. Know and prepare for it like a warrior going into battle.

Catch the first, tiniest instance. By the time you realize you've been triggered, it's often too late: you've said something you regret, you've sunk into a mood, or you've lost your composure. But your reactions give advance warning. You only have to train yourself to notice it. Before the storm blows in, there are small signs, little puffy wisps of clouds on an otherwise blue sky. Like spotting the clouds that precede a weather front, you can learn how to track these tiny signals before they unfold into full-blown reactions.

The minuscule signals preceding a violent reaction are creeping feelings of fear, aggravation, or frozenness. Becoming sensitive to your feelings and developing acute awareness of your emotional states is a learnable skill that can help you manage your emotional responses. If you can catch the tiniest, first little feeling, you create a wedge—a small but significant distance between you and your emotional response. This wedge gives you time, a little breathing room to manage yourself and to choose your response. Maybe you use the time to take a short walk around to calm down, count to ten, call a friend, or just breathe. Each of us will have our own method, but the value lies in our ability to protect ourselves from getting kidnapped by our emotions. With enough practice, you can use the early warning signals of your emotional states to postpone your immediate reaction and make a thoughtful choice about how to respond.

Have your feelings and have compassion for them. Triggers set off emotions, and many of us are afraid of our emotions, especially sadness, fear, and pain. Triggers link us back to an early hurt, an old wound we still have a lot of feelings about. But being afraid of emotions constitutes a major power leak. When you fight against your emotions, you fight *two* battles: one against the emotions associated with old wounds, and one against the stress of the emotions you're currently engaged in—what you're feeling in the moment. The more you feel you need to defend or protect against something in yourself, the more vulnerable you become.

One of the keys to personal power is openness to your feelings, or, in other words, self-compassion. Feelings are difficult enough—especially feelings related to our core wounds. If you repress your feelings, however, put yourself down for feeling them, or try to hide them, you get tangled up even worse.

Hating our emotions means hating ourselves and, accordingly, losing rank. It's a state that makes you defensive and rigid. When you are afraid of your feelings, you become afraid of others for fear they could provoke a response, making you feel even more vulnerable. Whenever you don't own your feelings, your feelings own you.

Accepting your feelings is an act of self-compassion. Compassion softens us, opens us up to our experience, and thus, gives us flexibility. When we are flexible, like bamboo, we can bend in the storm. We won't break. We can go with what happens without resistance. We are neither stiff with self-hatred and shame, nor frozen with fear. It takes self-development to get there, but the payoff—the ability to surf the waves of your emotional seas—is immeasurable.

Doable Practice #2: Tame Your Triggers

Look back over your day, and take a "trigger inventory." Do this every day for a week, and see what effect it has. Review your day and notice what set you off. Did anything make you feel, even momentarily, disempowered? Remember: triggers indicate something about you, and not necessarily the other person. Your answers should reflect an internal —not external—feeling. Did you react in a way you wish you hadn't? Write down the places, people, events, issues that knocked you off balance, and the responses you had to them.

Now, choose one, and without thinking too much about it, see if you can retrospectively do two things: first, were you able to identify the tiniest signal of your reaction before it escalated? Second, still thinking retrospectively, what could you have done to calm yourself, or regain your center, after having gotten triggered?

Guideline #3: Beware of Foreign Entanglements

Abraham Lincoln's life was filled with failure, hardship, and loss. His mother died when he was nine years old. Ten years later, his sister died in childbirth. Ann Rutledge, his first real love, died of typhoid, leaving Lincoln in a severe depression. Before winning the presidency, he failed in eight elections. He lost two of his four sons while he was alive. His years as president during the Civil War were some of the toughest any president had endured. Perhaps unsurprisingly, he was not a popular president and had many enemies. He said that if by the end of his term, "I have lost every other friend on earth, I shall at least have one friend left, and that friend shall be down inside of me."

As social animals, we walk a fine line between belonging and independence, between seeking the love of others and betraying ourselves to please them. We want and need to be loved by our community, but doing so at the expense of our freedom weakens us. The more we care what others think, the more we place our self-perceived power in the hands of others. Our sense of power drops. To have personal power, we need to risk standing alone. We need to be able to endure the tension between following what we know is right and losing the support of others. We must be able to be open to the love of others, but we also must be able to survive if we lose it. When Nelson Mandela was in prison, he kept a piece of paper in his cell, printed with the following words from William Ernest Henley's poem "Invictus": "I am the master of my fate: I am the captain of my soul."

Here is the upside of disinhibition. Remember, as we saw in Chapter 1, that high-power individuals are more immune from peer pressure. They are willing to step outside the box of social convention. Fitting in and going along with the crowd may give you momentary popularity, even increase your social rank, but it won't help you grow your personal power.

One way we become entangled—that is, inhibited—is by needing others to ratify our opinion, rank, or feelings. We get angry when others disagree with us. We don't just state our opinion; we insist on it. We become argumentative. Or, we seek allies to bolster our side, and gossip about the adversary, seeking to discredit them. These behaviors stem from feeling undervalued. We take another's differing opinion as a criticism or rejection, and then either attack them for it or collapse, unable to stand alone with our opinion. We lose the respect of others when we try to force their agreement.

Several years back, I had a client who supervised an agency. She was terrific in her job, working with her staff one-to-one on their caseloads. But when it came to running meetings, she struggled mightily. Her staff complained about her style, especially her aggressiveness. But as she explained to me, she didn't intend to be aggressive. And she didn't understand what went wrong during meetings. So, she invited me to sit in on one. Afterwards, she asked me for feedback.

"What did you see?" she asked. I told her it appeared that she presented her ideas *against* the other ideas. She didn't offer direction or suggestions, but argued against the validity of others' input. She was stunned. She didn't realize what she'd been doing.

As we discussed and explored further, she found out she felt she had something to prove. She felt one-down. She didn't think others valued her contributions. In fact, before she even spoke, she anticipated that her contributions would be rejected or devalued. Thus, she didn't start at a neutral place. She began already convinced she was discredited and came into the conversation fighting against a perceived sense of low worth.

Whenever we feel that our power needs to be ratified by others, or, as in the case of my client, not ratified by others, we place our self-worth in their hands, allowing our behavior to be dictated by their praise and criticisms. When coupled with our positional power, this tendency makes for difficult dynamics and puts unfair pressure on those over whom we have power. We've all experienced it from the other side: bosses who get insulted when subordinates disagree, teachers who need students' respect or adoration, parents who feel offended when their child chooses a path different from their own.

To grow your personal power, you need to stand for your own ideas without forcing others to agree with or share your point of view. People who use power well offer their opinion; they don't insist on it.

Wean yourself off the praise of others. As a leader or someone in a position of power, you face no shortage of feedback as to how you should or shouldn't be operating. If you're famous, or have a significant public profile, all you have to do is open a newspaper or go online and read about yourself. Everyone has an idea about what you should do, how you should have done it, and what you shouldn't have done.

When I speak and lecture, I am on the receiving end of unsolicited advice. When I first started out, I was very keen to hear praise. I was eager to read the feedback forms, gobbling up all the affirmative things I could read about myself. But, over time, I noticed two phenomena: First, I never remembered the positive feedback. It felt good but didn't stay with me. Second, I would argue (to myself, internally) with negative feedback. I found myself indulging in a classic "attribution error": I would agree with the positive feedback, but disagree with the negative feedback.

One day, it hit me: I can't have it both ways. If I don't like criticism, I can't like praise, either. I can't have my cake and eat it too.

I didn't have a problem just hearing negative feedback. The bigger problem I had was disconnection from my own, meaningful benchmarks. I wasn't considering the things that mattered to me. The praise didn't stick because it didn't really mean anything after the initial self-esteem boost wore off. I realized that praise meant working for the goals of others.

Right then and there, on the spot, I decided I wanted neither praise nor feedback, unless I deliberately sought it out. And if I did, I would define what I wanted in the feedback. Now, when someone says they appreciated something I've done, I say, "I'm glad you liked it," and then ask, "What did you like about it?" to make explicit their benchmark for my performance. What someone else thinks is good about me is a reflection of their values, not mine.

True excellence is not excelling at what someone else determines is valuable. You have to define success for yourself. To become free of entanglement with others' opinions, you must set your own benchmarks for success as well as failure. Be open to feedback, but also work towards the goals, praise, and outcomes that are defined by you, meaningful to you, and agreed with by you. It's useful to have feedback, and to be open to what people think, but not without first explicating the criterion in their feedback. Otherwise, you orient yourself to values that may not be yours.

Doable Practice #3: Beware of Foreign Entanglements

Each day, as soon as you wake up, take three to five minutes and write down your benchmarks for success that day. What small, bite-sized things do you want to accomplish today that will make you feel like you succeeded, according to *your* definition of success? This practice will help you focus on what's valuable to you, according to you. It's not about projects or tasks, but your own personal growth goals. Make sure the behavior goals you have for the day aren't vague or overly ambitious (e.g. count to ten before responding, ask for help, make one suggestion at a meeting).

Do this each day for a week, and see what you notice. Check in with yourself after a week, and see how you're doing.

How have you lived up to your internal benchmarks? Do they serve you? Do they need to be adjusted?

Guideline # 4: Love Your Low Rank

Ben Horowitz, Silicon Valley technology advisor and investor, sold his company, Opsware, to Hewlitt Packard for $1.6 billion in cash when he was forty-one years old. That looks like a success if all you know is how the story ended. But his was a harrowing, white-knuckle ride. At the lowest point in his journey, shares for his company plummeted to thirty-five cents each.

In a candid book detailing what he learned in the process, Horowitz describes his fear, doubt, and moments of crippling anxiety during his tenure as CEO. Of all the strenuous lessons he had to learn, he says nothing compared to the burden of managing his own psychology, of "keeping [his] mind in check." He wonders why no one else talks about what he jokingly refers to as "the fight club of management":[2]

> Over the years, I've spoken to hundreds of CEOs, all with the same experience. Nonetheless, very few people talk about it and I have never read anything on the topic. It's like the fight club of management: the first rule of the CEO psychological meltdown is don't talk about the psychological meltdown.[3]

Regardless of social position, we all have low-rank moments. Low rank causes vulnerability: from being a beginner, to not knowing, needing help, and having a meltdown. Feelings of low rank are an indispensable facet of the human equation, and if we hate it in ourselves, we put our authority in jeopardy.

At the lowest point, when it looked like his company wouldn't survive, Horowitz decided to share his struggles with his team. At first he was afraid that appearing vulnerable and weak would frighten people away, that he would lose their trust and they would quit. Instead, the opposite happened: people became engaged and were able to collaborate on a solution together. Working side by side, they kept the company intact, turned it around, and, well, you know the happy ending.

Loving low rank is an act of utter faith. You have to embrace the hard things as they're happening—the low moments, the tough roles you're in. But to do so brings unparalleled rewards. We source much of our personal power from the most difficult times in life. And if we turn against our low rank, we lose that precious superpower.

To love your low rank, you must remember to embrace your vulnerability, and embrace the experiences in your low-rank roles.

Embrace your vulnerability. Nothing makes you more vulnerable than the inability to be vulnerable. If you cannot fail, cannot be wrong, cannot make a mistake, you are a sitting duck. Your inviolable strength comes from your willingness to have nothing to lose. If you can't lose an argument, walk away from a disagreement, admit defeat, or apologize for a mistake, you have placed your feelings of worth in the hands of another and are completely open to manipulation.

Fear of vulnerability leads us to use power poorly: we hide mistakes, don't ask for help, and push forward without knowledge or resources. We would rather drive in circles than stop and ask for directions. An inability to be vulnerable is a universal sign of low personal power. It's the reason people swagger, act invincible, and play the tough guy. But the façade eventually crumbles. While bad managers abhor vulnerability for fear of appearing weak, good managers like Horowitz use vulnerability as a tool to build trust and meaningful relationships.

Embrace the power in low rank. If you have completed your Power-print exercise, this will sound familiar. Low-rank challenges are the source of some of your greatest strengths and powers. Your personal power comes from your struggles, those life experiences that were not easy. Personal power is grown through the hard work of self-development, of managing misfortune, turning around failure, and working through discrimination and internalized oppression or a challenging childhood.

Low rank—not just high rank—is where you can find many of your robust powers. Don't undervalue the insights you discover in your lowest-ranking roles. When you have less to lose, when you are ill-equipped and inexperienced, your lack of status allows you to see things with clarity, to entertain ideas others can't and take risks others won't.

A common reaction to low rank is to try to gain status and leave behind the low-ranking role. But without compassion for where we've been, we could turn against the victim part of ourselves, as well as others in a similar position. When we don't appreciate our own suffering and deny the value of our low-rank experiences, we deny others' low rank as well. As a person wielding power, if you lack compassion towards yourself, you lack insight into those with lower rank.

It also creates a blind spot in our own use of power. As we keep striving for high rank, our gaze is perpetually skywards—up the ladder to those above. Climbing toward the top, we forget that we, too, have some power. The more we cast our gaze upwards, the more possible it is to forget where we have rank over others. We are prone to abusing our power over others when we forget our own rank. Prizing high rank over low rank can make us more likely to act or react from a "one-down" position, and misuse the power we have over others. Remember the first rule of power: *we act on how we feel*. Hating low rank keeps us in a victim identity, and thus, we forget our own rank and its responsibilities.

Doable Practice #4: Love Your Low Rank

Make a daily habit of looking back over the day, and noting down the different moments when you felt vulnerable, unsure, or unskilled. These are your low-rank moments. For each moment, ask yourself what you learned about yourself. Consider sharing your learning with someone whom you trust.

Guideline #5: Overestimate Your Rank and Underestimate Your Opponent's

This seems to be the opposite of conventional wisdom, which dictates you should never underestimate your opponent. But your true enemy is placing yourself in one-down position.

Think about a power struggle. As tempting as it is to enter a power struggle, the minute you've entered into one, you've already lost. In a struggle for power, you define yourself as the other person's equal, or as someone with lower rank, because they have something you need. When you fight over anything—whether it's love, behavior, obedience, involvement in a project, an operational budget, seat at the conference table, parking space, or a toy—you are not in control of the thing you want. When you participate in a power struggle, you play a game with an uncertain outcome, cede control, and commit all your resources. It's your personal *realpolitik*; using power to keep your power. You become locked in a positive feedback loop escalating out of control. To win, you have to continually raise the stakes until you're pushed to capitulate or reward your opponent. Neither is a legitimate form of power.

A power struggle is, by definition, a competition between social *equals*. Parents don't have power struggles with children. Bosses don't have power struggles with employees, and teachers don't have power struggles with students. It's better to walk away without your momentary goals satisfied than to enter into an argument or fight over them.

And yet we enter power struggles unwittingly all the time. Whenever we underestimate our power and overestimate the other's, we are in a power struggle. In my role as a coach and consultant, I've seen it as an epidemic. Conflict almost always begins and escalates when both parties believe the other has more power. When you're convinced the opponent has greater ammunition, you bring a bigger gun yourself. You anticipate you'll need more firepower than you have, believing yourself to be in the one-down or "underdog" position.

Imagine you have to have a difficult conversation with a colleague, and you're afraid of their response. So you steel yourself, gird your loins, get all your facts and figures straight, and shoot from the hip. But instead of seeming competent and confident, you come across as arrogant and aggressive, and offend the other person.

This is also how and why many performance conversations fail. Feeling unequal to the task, the manager tries to get the conversation over with, using data as "proof" to hold off any reaction or resistance on the other side. The manager feels like she's in a low-rank position relative to the tasks of the performance management process and doesn't see how she comes across as an aggressor. From the other's point of view, it's a traumatic experience.

Whenever you find yourself in contention with someone else, assume you have greater rank than your opponent. It doesn't mean you think less of the person. It doesn't mean being patronizing or controlling. It means you assume the other person views you as having greater rank.

Here's why and how it's important:

When you overestimate your rank, you don't come from a low-rank (limbic) position. When we overestimate the other person's power, we automatically put ourselves in a low-rank position relative to them. We feel at the mercy of their control, and this triggers a limbic state. As we give control over to our emotions, we lose touch with the abilities we've fostered over time. When we feel we have higher rank, we don't fear the other. We act with more benevolence and generosity. Our mind at ease, we act in alignment with qualities that matter to us, and we feel more relaxed as a result.

Think of yourself as having power even when you don't feel it. We all have some authority, somewhere, in some aspect of our lives. Connecting with your personal power reveals to you the influential abilities you really do have. It also gives you insight into how the other sees you: you might be surprised at how powerful you look to others.

You find powers you didn't consider. I was working with a client, Roger, who had a great deal of trouble with a domineering co-worker. I asked Roger what power he had that his co-worker didn't. He thought for a moment, and then replied, "Well, no one really likes my co-worker, and I am well-liked at work." This gave him a revolutionary insight into their struggle. Roger not only felt more generous and compassionate, but he also found ways he could influence his co-worker, based on his greater power and his co-worker's weakness.

There is an inherent kernel of truth when you overestimate your rank. Think about it: if someone has a conflict with you, they must find you threatening in some way. They must see you as having some kind of higher rank. Unless they're just a bully, there's something about you they find intimidating, frightening, difficult, or powerful. Give it some thought: What makes you a formidable foe? What power do you have that you are neglecting to remember?

You can de-escalate the conflict. When convinced we're the weaker party, we implement additional force. When the other person does the same, it's an instantaneous escalation and a zero-sum game: one side loses and one side wins. But there's no real winner in a power struggle, because you have to continually up the ante until you run out of resources.

When we think we have higher rank, however, we don't have to defend, attack, or protect. In a more powerful state, we are not threatened. We are not reactive. We have options and choices. Our lack of defensiveness allows us to de-escalate the situation. We have the freedom and spaciousness to step away, consider our next move, or even to do nothing at all. Ultimately, it doesn't matter what we do: simply not reacting defensively or protectively is an automatic de-escalation unto itself.

Doable Practice #5: Overestimate Your Rank
and Underestimate Your Opponent's

If you feel caught in a struggle with someone or something, take three minutes and do this: imagine yourself as much, much older and wiser—as someone who has achieved all you've wanted in life. Imagine you have all that you need to be well, to feel well, and nothing can threaten you. Let yourself imagine this, and as you do, breathe into it. Feel it, until you enter the state of mind of this wiser, future you. This enables you to overestimate your rank, to increase your inner feelings of rank relative to the other person or thing.

When you feel ready, and calmed by this imagination, imagine yourself responding to the struggle or conflict from this state of mind. Write down what you notice from this reflection. Is there a certain behavior you can take with you into the conflict next time? Is there a small thing you can do to respond without getting caught in the power struggle?

We have now come to the end of the central guidelines for growing your personal power and cultivating your traits. This is the first step in becoming more powerful and influential, and using your power in beneficial ways.

But there's more. Using power with others effectively means gaining their respect. The next two chapters outline the guidelines for using your power legitimately, how to gain and keep the respect of others, and how to use your power in your organizations and groups so that you create healthy power cultures.

6

Use Your Personal Power

If your actions inspire others to dream more,
learn more, do more and become more, you are a leader.
—JOHN QUINCY ADAMS

You can get the money, you can get the power,
but keep your eyes on, the final hour.
—LAURYN HILL

O nce upon a time, there lived a king. One day, the king's astrologer warned that a magical rainstorm was coming and that the rainwater would turn people mad if they drank it. The king, equipped with this knowledge, implored his people not to drink the water. But they did anyway, and true to the astrologer's word, all went mad. The king, distraught that his people had all lost their minds, had no choice but to drink it too. As the only sane person in a kingdom of lunatics, he would be the crazy one, so he decided to keep his crown by joining his subjects in their madness.

A fable, yes, but an apt metaphor for a truism about power: the authority of a role resides in the people. We can sit on the throne, but without people's willingness to follow us, we have no authority. Legitimacy is something we earn by gaining the other's respect. People don't obey us because we are the leader; we are the leader when people follow us. In the case of the king, it means meeting the people where they are.

In light of the lessons in previous chapters, you may wonder how the subjects of a king, or any leader for that matter, could choose not to follow the person in charge. Don't followers automatically adjust to the person commanding a room? Isn't power a self-fulfilling prophecy—people respond to and even reify our rank? Certainly —to an extent. Power changes how people perceive you, but it doesn't mean they will follow you, or do your bidding. Your authority has to be earned. People may ask for your autograph, but they may not obey your decree. This chapter focuses on using power. Actually wielding power adds another level of complexity to the picture. How people see you and project onto you doesn't translate into being effective. To be effective, you need to use your power legitimately.

In the last chapter, we focused on rules for growing and cultivating your personal power. Developing your in-sourced power is the first step. The next step is using it legitimately, in a way in which people ratify it without being coerced to do so. Your ability to influence others depends on being able to gain the respect of others. Respect cannot be taken; it has to flow freely from the hearts of those who follow.

It's a profound paradox of power: although a position of power comes with the means to enforce it (demoting employees, suspending students, grounding children, jailing dissenters), if you use those means to get people to obey you, you undermine your legitimacy. The position that you occupy, and which authorizes you to exert power, only gives you legitimacy on paper. Unless those who follow you recognize your authority, your power is felt to be illegitimate. The law doesn't sanction your power—the people do.

Whenever we exert authority through coercion or force, we lose legitimacy and become despotic, resulting in an increasingly tenuous hold over people. When this happens at the level of state, when a leader loses the consent of the governed, that leader finds themselves in a very shaky position. There are three choices: a) step down, like Mikhail Gorbachev did when the Soviet Union dissolved and he lost the support of the government; b) fight and use the lethal force at their disposal, similar to how former Egyptian president Hosni Mubarak or Syrian president Bashar al-Assad plunged their countries into civil wars and decades of brutal dictatorship; or c) try to re-establish authority through legitimate means, as did South African president Frederik Willem de Klerk, who initiated the end of apartheid, decriminalized the African National Congress, and released Nelson Mandela from prison.

What happens at the individual level? Someone may have a designated position, but not respect. Without respect, they have no influence, can't make an impact, and aren't able to get things done. If you resort to coercion and force, you become, at best, bureaucratic and officious. At worst, you're tyrannical and dictatorial.

How do we get around this paradox? How do we get others to follow us, if we can't use—or use only lightly—the power that comes with our position?

To make your power effective and legitimate, you have to influence others through your own actions. Your behavior is your best influencing tool. But here's the thing: you are already influencing others, all the time. Everything you do and don't do, say and don't say, sends a message, and that message either positively or negatively influences people. You cannot *not* influence. The question is not how do you influence, but rather, how are you *already* influencing people? What impact are you already making with the power you already have?

Do you know about the Johari Window? It is a technique designed to help people better understand themselves and their relationships with others.[1] There are four quadrants in the Johari Window: what we know and don't know about ourselves, and what others know and don't know about us. The upper right hand corner of the following diagram is our *blind spot*: the parts of ourselves we are not aware of, but which others perceive.

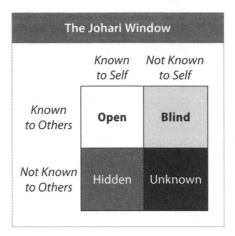

Figure 6.1

When it comes to influencing others, we often operate in our blind spot, unaware of the impact we're making. Feelings drive behavior, as we've seen, but we're often unaware of them, and by extension, of our self-perceived rank and power. Influencing others and doing so while being seen as legitimate starts and ends with mastering sensations that often exist in the realm of our unconscious: our feelings, our sense of power, and the messages we convey about ourselves. The following guidelines for using power legitimately focus on your behavior, self-awareness, and awareness of the other:

Guideline #6: Say Goodbye to Being "Just Me"

Several years ago, I took on the job of Director of Training at the Process Work Institute, the graduate school where I taught. I was a month or so into my role, and as I was walking down the hallway one day, I saw a good friend walking towards me. We stopped and chatted, and she asked me, "How does it feel to be the boss?"

I thought she meant it lightheartedly, so I said, "It's mostly just a lot of work." But she looked at me, and grew serious.

"You have a lot of authority now," she said. "You could fire me." I wasn't sure how to respond. Truthfully, I was stunned. I laughed awkwardly, and mumbled something like, "Well, that's not what's on my mind."

As I walked away, I felt terrible because she spoke to my role, but not to me, her friend. I wanted to protest, "Hey, it's me! I'm the same person I was before!" I was puzzled that she would make such a big deal about my job, but I also felt loss—the loss of "just me," my "normal identity."

Positional power is a social identity that changes how people relate to us. High rank is a commodity, a symbol, and an identity, and people have a vast array of responses to it. In a high-ranking role, we are subject to all kinds of projections, attacks, flattery, and requests. We don't know whether people are truly interested in us or merely what we can provide for them. We can become a means to an end or a symbol of oppression and dominance. Whatever people project onto you, you are no longer just "you," the individual. You occupy a social role that carries social meaning.

The challenges here are numerous. You are subject to social stereotyping, misattribution, flattery, as well as attacks and criticisms that can be truly awful. Stepping into a high-ranking, public role is not for the faint of heart. It can be difficult to bear, but can also lead you astray if you take it personally. There are several methods to stay grounded when inhabiting a high-ranking role:

Don't take it personally. A high-ranking social role—a role of power—is a public process. Public roles such as mayor, professional athlete, pop cultural figure, or celebrity combine position, fame, and social status others grant *en masse*. Whenever we step into a visibly high-ranking role, we take a risk: we become part of the public discourse.

For every single person who assumes that risk and sacrifices anonymity, there are hundreds of critics ready to take aim. In a world of social media and 24/7-scrutiny, managing the role and its critics is harder than ever before. The anonymity and instantaneity of social media is like living in an echo chamber: everything we do and say is instantly amplified, distorted, taken out of context, and used against us. Sometimes it's adoration, but often it's criticism and, frequently, it's hate. Public figures receive harassment, bullying, and death threats on a daily basis.

Dave Chappelle, a comedic genius, ran one of the most successful television shows on the air. In the middle of it all, he walked away. He left a five-year, $50 million dollar contract, and a brilliant career behind because, as he put it, "people laughed in the wrong way." In conversation with author and activist Maya Angelou, he explained, "When I left my show, it was because I did this sketch, and I knew what I intended, but somebody laughed differently than what I intended. And I caught it. ... And it was painful." Chappelle's perception drove him to leave the public eye. He said, "I don't want to be co-opted or subverted. I don't want to be my own worst enemy or be used against myself. That's what happens to famous people."[2]

Some leaders' experience of prejudice is amplified by additional stereotypes related to their social identity and appearance: as black, for instance, or female, gay, Muslim, disabled, and so on (see the section in Chapter 8, titled "Breaking Down Barriers"). Additional negative stereotyping makes being in a public role even more of a challenge, and can have serious consequences on physical and emotional health, as well as self-esteem and performance.

While it's important to grow a thick skin, being stereotyped is painful and has a real cost. If you compartmentalize at the exclusion of other coping techniques—if you simply repress the hurt you feel or pretend it doesn't bother you—you can become bitter, resentful, or even ill. Better strategies include fostering self-compassion, understanding the difference between you and the projections people put on you, and having a circle of close friends who care for you.

When others stereotype you in your role, it can feel like a loss of your personal identity. But you don't have to join in. You can hold onto your individuality, complexity, and inner power. Remember:

1) Don't let the role define you. Embrace your multiple identities; others may not be able to, but you should. Your social identity and role are facets of the full you. Appreciate all the roles you play, all the different social circles you live in, and the different places and ways you show up in the world—as you.

2) Projections define the person projecting, not the target. When the first female prime Minister of Australia, Julia Gillard, was criticized for her policies, her opposition used sexist and misogynist epithets. Others' perceptions have to do with their own issues; stereotypes of your social identity reflect people's limited and narrow worldview. It's their problem, not yours.

3) Be prepared for it. Know that it's "part of the job," and also part of history. Humanity is engaged in a long and at times violent struggle about power. When you step into a position of authority, you are assuming a role in that long and painful drama.

4) Affirm yourself on your own terms. Think about the skills, attributes, and abilities that matter to you. Remember your values and beliefs, and what you deem important. Continually assess yourself on those areas that matter most to you. Affirm yourself for living up to the standards you set for yourself.

Don't be dazzled by the archetype. Negative stereotypes hurt, but there are also positive projections, and we can also be lured into identifying with the more-than-human aspects others believe our roles entail. During the 2008 Democratic Party presidential primaries, then-candidate Barack Obama told a reporter:

> I had become a symbol for the next thing. So some of it was undeserved, but what it told me was that people really were looking for something different. ... I joked with my team—and it wasn't entirely a joke, it's something I still think about— that the country was looking for a Barack Obama. Now, I'm not sure that I *am* Barack Obama, right? But they were looking for an idea like that.[3]

When you step into a public role, you become a symbol, not just a person. Barack Obama felt it: he was himself, and also had become an idea. High-ranking roles of any kind are symbols for something larger than life; they are archetypes of greatness. I remember being six years old and seeing my 1st grade teacher in the grocery store. I was dumbfounded. I couldn't imagine my teacher *eating food*! In my six-year-old mind, teachers didn't cook or eat. They were, after all, teachers—the role, and idea of teachers.

Josef Ackermann, former CEO of Deutsche Bank, described the first time he realized he had become a role rather than an individual: Right after Ackermann ascended to CEO, a colleague—the former chief of Deutsche Bundesbank—took him aside and told him, "From now on, you must remember that you are two people. You are the person whom you and your friends know, but you are also a symbol for something. Never confuse the two. Don't take criticism of the symbol as criticism of the person."[4] When you are a symbol, you will be admired and respected. But as Obama and others have learned, you will also be judged against the archetype and vilified for not living up to it.

The legendary psychologist Carl Jung called the larger-than-life facets of roles *archetypes*. An archetype is a symbol of collective qualities, a magnet that draws every conceivable projection toward it. Jung warned against the human tendency to identify with them. The archetypal quality of the role is like the ring of Mordor: it will devour whoever desires it.

The archetype of power is alluring, and contains multitudes of stature: protector, hero, rescuer, sovereign, guru. In an archetypal role, such as president or king, you can even feel like a god. But we give in to minor, everyday archetypes too. When parents fall into the aura of their archetype, they become over-protective. They hover over their children, interfere in their conflicts, protecting them from challenges, and depriving them of the opportunity to develop independence and resilience.

Bosses who identify with the sovereign aspect of power micro-manage others and refuse to believe anyone can accomplish things as well as they can. When doctors decline to consult with others or ask for help, or get defensive when a patient asks for a second opinion, they have fallen prey to the godlike feelings of infallibility. Therapists over-identify with the "hero" or "rescuer" aspect of their roles when they believe they are indispensable, and thus become enmeshed in the lives of their clients, fomenting their clients' dependency and vulnerability. When a social activist sacrifices their health and relationships to save the world, they have become absorbed by the savior or warrior archetype.

It's tempting, and unfortunately very easy, to be dazzled by the people's positive projections and believe their admiration and respect is meant for you. Once you believe in the greatness of the archetype, however, you lose your compass. You begin to act out of your desire to uphold the image, and not out of your genuine desire to do what's right. To guard against this, you need to share the role.

Share the role. Though you may feel it belongs to you and you alone, your high-ranking role is public property.[5] Many people have held the role before you stepped in, and many more will occupy it after you're gone. You are not your role. Identifying with it will dangerously inflate your ego and allow you to stray off-course from your values. By believing yourself to embody the archetype, you force those around you into complementary positions relative to the role. Overly protective parents create incompetent, overly reliant children. Dominant leaders create compliant and disempowered employees who don't think for themselves. The teacher who overdoes the expert role disengages his students from their own process of discovery and learning. The therapist who clings to the role of healer compels her clients to be unwell so she can feel helpful, thus creating an unhealthy dynamic of dependence.

Inhabiting a role responsibly means sharing its "public properties" with others. The archetypal elements of a role—heroism, righteousness, wisdom—are behaviors and attitudes that belong to all. Teachers share the role when they support their students' idiosyncratic thinking, when they encourage students to teach each other, and when they admit when they don't have the answer. Bosses share their role by empowering their teams, encouraging subordinates to take on leadership roles, and mentoring employees. Coaches share the role by supporting their players to motivate and encourage each other. All of these are the necessary undertakings of good leadership. Children need to learn responsibility, team members need to think like the boss, clients need to access their own capacity to work through their problems. If we "hog" the role, we neglect our duty to develop those around us, and moreover, disallow them from doing the work themselves.

Another way to share the role is to give credit. When people over-identify with power, they fail to acknowledge others' contributions. No one springs forth, fully developed, into a role. Nor does anyone attain a role of authority without the help, support, insights, and contributions of those around them. It's too easy for the one with highest rank to take all the credit. Public adoration, coupled with society's tendency to deify leaders, creates the false sense that a leader somehow invents, develops, or creates success singlehandedly. But success, even inadvertent success, is always a team effort. Good ideas come from shared discussions, informal conversation, and interaction. Sharing the role means giving credit, noticing how and when others contribute, mentoring others to assume aspects of the leadership role (even from within their current position), and above all, acknowledging contributors publicly.

Respect your authority. While some people can over-identify with their role, others need to take theirs more seriously. Sometimes we resist the rank and associated authority that comes with our role, minimizing our difference from others, or intimidated by latitude our rank provides. We want to be part of the group, as I did when I became Director of Training. I just wanted to be "me," the same old Julie I'd always been. I wanted my friends and colleagues to treat me like they always had.

But it's just not possible. People see rank, and you have to accept it. You have to try to anticipate how others will perceive and respond to your position. When you step into a role of power, you give up the luxury of being "normal," because the rank and authority of your role magnify everything you do. Being unaware of this fact, or resisting it, can actually lead to misuse of power.

Here's how: When you have power, you become a *program*, not a *person*.[6] People subject to your authority interpret your actions as a set of implicit behavioral rules, a default norm others will mimic or resist. The teacher's way of speaking and thinking becomes the implicit default. The boss's approach to conflict becomes the department's de-facto conflict approach. The parent's lifestyle choices, from how and when meals are eaten to how the neighbors are discussed at the dinner table, become normal—the right way to live.

What you think of as your "mere presence," how those around you perceive you, is also often diametrically opposed to what you intend. When you think you're inviting others to speak, they feel put on the spot. You think you're easing the atmosphere, but they think you're making light of a serious situation and avoiding difficult topics. In a meeting, you try to stick to the agenda so you don't waste everyone's valuable time, and yet someone accuses you of suppressing conversation.

You cannot *not* have a personal style. We all do. It's human nature to have preferences and predictable patterns of behaviors, such as ways of speaking, relating to others, and getting things done. When you add rank to the mix, your personal style becomes a leadership style. People interpret your approach as the behavior others should follow. Even if it's not a formalized rule, it becomes one of the values that creates contextual rank. Those who approximate the leader's style or behaviors best, have more rank. There are real consequences to this. Leaders tend to be fond of those who are most like them. It's an unconscious bias, a preference based on comfort and mirroring. Those who think like us, relate like us, and behave like us are just easier to get along with.

It's important to be aware of your rank's unconscious influences, and to respect the authority you wield. If you minimize it, try to be equals, or don't acknowledge the dynamic, you could unwittingly play favorites, or sideline others who don't mesh with your style. If you value freedom and diversity, and if it's important to you that people think and act for themselves, then do the following:

1) Ask yourself: Do people speak freely around you? How often do you hear opinions different from your own? When you give an opinion, or make a statement, do people engage with it, or go silent and back off?

2) Don't be naïve. Know that your way of being will be seen as dominant, whether you intend it to be or not.

3) Meta-communicate—that is, talk about the way you talk— about your style, however it manifests: speaking, writing, thinking, engaging with conflict, et cetera. Do this by making

self-referential comments, indicating that you recognize your style, that it is but one style among many, and that others have different styles that are equally important to share.

4) Communicate to others that you appreciate different ways of thinking, talking, and interacting.

5) If you're giving instructions, be sure to differentiate the "what" from the "how." It's easy to slip into the habit of telling people *how* to do things when all you need is to tell them *what* to do. Acknowledge there are many paths to get there, and your way is just one.

6) Acknowledge and appreciate other styles when you see them being used.

Doable Practice #6: Say Goodbye to Being "Just Me"

How do you, your role, and others' expectations shape how you think of yourself as a leader? How do you understand and navigate the different experiences you have in a high-power role: your personal identity, the qualities of the role, and how others see you in that role? On a piece of paper, draw three columns.

Write "THE ROLE" on top of column one and write down those properties and qualities that belong to your role (coach, parent, pastor, teacher, boss) and which you think are the most important qualities of the role (that is, for anyone who would fill it in, as they belong to the role itself).

In column two, entitled "YOU," write down those qualities that you *personally* bring to the role, your own traits and qualities. Note where the qualities in column one and two are the same, and where they diverge.

Next, in column three, entitled "OTHERS," write down how you think others perceive you in that role. What qualities and traits do you think they see in you?

This exercise would be enough for you to gain insights into yourself, your role, and how you think others see you. But if you can, go one step further, and ask a friend, coach, or advisor to fill it out for you as well, and then compare your answers. What did you discover about yourself? What's consistent between the role you play, your own qualities, and how others see you? How accurate were you in your assessment? Do you feel you need to make any adjustments to be more aligned with your own qualities, or perhaps to be more, or less sensitive to what others see?

Guideline #7: If You Use It, You Lose It

A friend of mine who consults with church leaders cautions new priests, "Don't use power until you have it." She finds that one of the problems with newly appointed leaders is that they use the power of their position before they have gained legitimacy—that is, before people follow them from their hearts. It takes time to become a leader, even if the sign above your door reads "CEO" or "professor" or "pastor." My friend shared with me the story of Aaron, a priest who had recently been called to his first position as rector at an Episcopal Church.[7]

Aaron was excited to have his own congregation. He planned to make some changes to bring the church up to date. First among these changes was to close off the back rows of the church, in order to make people sit closer together up front. He saw that people in this congregation weren't as engaged with each other as they could be, and he wanted to enhance the feeling of community among worshippers.

Aaron knew that people had become used to sitting with their own family, somewhat separate from other congregants, but he assumed a stronger feeling of community would mitigate any objection.

In the first week of his tenure, he closed off the rows without discussing the change with the vestry or announcing it to the congregation. He was unprepared for the response.

The vestry was annoyed they hadn't been consulted. Many of the older members of the church were offended. They also happened to be some of the wealthier and established families, and threatened to leave the church. After all, they had been members before Aaron took on his role. By presuming he knew how to run *their* church better, Aaron trampled their sense of ownership and stewardship over their faith community. To them, his behavior was not only annoying, but insulting and disrespectful of their lived commitment to their church and each other.

The pushback Aaron received completely blindsided him. He interpreted it as a challenge to his leadership. His response was to dig in and hold onto his position, fearing that if he capitulated, he would lose his authority. He defended the move, explaining the value of creating more communal feelings. But things went from bad to worse, and Aaron's first year at the church was spent in conflict. Having been outflanked with that initial significant decision, the vestry lost trust in him, and proceeded to question virtually every idea he had, even the good ones. In his frustration, Aaron fell prey to several outbursts of anger with members of the vestry. Eventually the Bishop was consulted, and the church engaged mediators to mend the situation. By then, it was too late. The Diocese had to help negotiate a severance package, and Aaron had to leave the congregation before he had time to figure out where he had gone wrong, or discern his next call to a new church.

Aaron didn't understand that authority was something earned, and not a quality that comes automatically with the position. Just as I had discovered in that 10th grade classroom, Aaron learned the hard way that just because your nametag reads "priest," "teacher," or "director," it doesn't mean you have legitimacy. People don't merely do what you say because you're the boss. You have to earn it.

The undoing of many a leader starts with using authority before gaining the trust and respect of others. They enter their new role with a laundry list of changes and an agenda of making a clean start. They feel they need to have some "wins" to distinguish themselves from the previous leader, and to prove they deserve to be in the position. So they act rashly and use the authority of their role before gaining others' trust.

Leaders who go down this path often find out it's the quickest route out the door.

Just because you *can* force people to do what you want doesn't mean you *should*. Your authority alone is not leadership. People need a reason to follow you; they need to know the rationale behind your agenda. Getting hired or even elected by a landslide doesn't promise people will follow you without you first gaining their buy-in.

If you don't take time to develop your influence, others will perceive you as autocratic and you'll lose their respect as a result. Your behavior, not the position, gives you legitimacy, and behavior needs time to make an impact. There is no shortcut to influence. It happens through contact, relationship, and trust-building.

How do you earn that respect?

Be a teacher. The real work of leaders is teaching. Leaders can't expect people to follow them without a reason. People need to understand the rationale behind an agenda, and the urgency behind a decision. They need to be informed in order to weigh the pros and cons of a decision. Above all, people like to feel engaged in the decisions that affect them.

Be a teacher by creating dialogue. Discuss ideas with people. Explain your thinking and listen to theirs. Give people time to think, digest, and object if necessary. Aaron should have held conversations and engaged the congregation about his concern for community. Leaders who use power well spend a lot of time reaching out to people, educating them about issues, securing support, and giving their supporters—and opponents—space and time to think about the consequences of decisions.

Leading has a lot in common with selling. Both salespeople and leaders have to make a case. A leader has to sell her ideas, and sell change, because people have sunk a lot of time, money, ego, and emotion into the status quo and need a worthwhile reason to change. Continuing an inefficient process is easier on us than learning a new, better way. As a salesperson, you wouldn't expect someone to buy what you're peddling just because you say it's a good product. The same is true for leading. You have to explain the value, demonstrate its usefulness, relate to others' concerns and "pain points," appreciate what people are already doing, and minimize, or prepare people for the effort and difficulty changing behavior entails.

Renew your authority ticket. During the Vietnam War, U.S. troops captured a young Việt Cộng soldier who, it turned out, had switched sides over the course of battle no fewer than five times. The U.S. infantrymen could hardly comprehend how, in a battle of territory and ideologies—of matters so near and dear to a person—someone could be disloyal to such an extent. When they asked him why, what made him switch sides, the Vietnamese soldier said it wasn't about territory or history. He was following leaders, he said, not ideas. And he followed whichever leader inspired him more. At one time, he venerated Ho Chi Minh, but when Ho failed to act in a virtuous manner, the soldier felt compelled to follow the leader on the other side of the battle.[8]

Earning the trust of others and gaining legitimacy for your authority is not a one-shot deal. Authority does not bestow a ticket valid for life. You need a new ticket for each ride. Your actions and decisions, as well as your outer circumstances, change how people feel. If people have given their consent to one of your decisions, if they've agreed to follow you once, it doesn't mean they'll get on the bus the next time. It's easy to confuse followership with loyalty. Like the Việt Cộng soldier, people are fickle. That's a good thing—it means they're critical thinkers. Thus, your authority needs to be ratified each time anew. You need to keep selling, and closing. Otherwise, if you assume people are on board, they'll quickly let you know they want to be asked.

Drink the rainwater. Remember the story of the king who drank the crazy-making rainwater so he could be with his people? "Drinking the rainwater" means this: "We're all in it together." This is not more than a platitude—it's an attitude and a belief that inspires trust and respect. People convey legitimacy to their leader when they feel their leader stands with them.

Another's poor performance reflects on your leadership ability. If your student fails, you have failed as a teacher. If your student doesn't pass the test, your teaching and guidance was insufficient. If your employee didn't deliver on something important, it could also be your failure as a boss for not setting him up to succeed. You cannot be critical of your subordinate without wondering what you did to contribute to their disappointing performance. If you have negative feedback for someone, you should have some for yourself, too.

This attitude gets reflected in how you speak. Is it "you" or is it "we?" Do you speak from within a struggle, or from the outside? Do you care about the outcomes personally, or do you solely berate and direct? How you speak begins with the feeling that you and others have a joint fate. Their success and failure belong to you as well.

Some of the most successful social activists I have seen use this way of thinking. When they speak to others, whether crowds of people or the media, they don't say "you" but "we." They don't criticize people, but include themselves as ones needing to be awakened.

Doable Practice #7: If You Use It, You Lose It

This exercise is an opportunity to practice gaining follower-ship without relying on authority alone. Think of something important you would like others' agreement or collaboration on. Try to summarize your vision or argument in no more than three sentences, stating why it's important and why others should buy into it. See if you can do it in the following way: a) stated in the positive, i.e., without debunking, criticizing, or refuting something else; and b) describing the benefits for the others, and for the greater good. Practice by yourself a few times and, if possible, with a confidante or friend. Ask for their feedback: not just about the content of your delivery, but how they experienced the energy and emotion behind the words.

Guideline #8: Do Your Job and Know Your Limits

When I was in graduate school at the University of Zurich, I had to endure a set of final exams that I thought would kill me. Nothing in my American high school or college experience prepared me for them. One was a set of hour-long oral exams with the professors in my three main subject areas. I feared most the one with Professor Strobl.

Strobl had been the head of the psychology department since before I was born, it seemed. Although a mild and friendly man, his knowledge of the field and stature intimidated me. He also had a thick Austrian accent I found incomprehensible. But most of all, I was scared I would blank out and forget a German term. I was comfortable with the English clinical terms and had to do a mental translation into the German. Under the pressure of the exam, it seemed easy to choke and forget the German.

Which, of course, I did. Strobl asked me to explain Freudian dream theory, and I froze. After about twenty seconds, which seemed like an eternity, I stammered an apology and explained that I knew the answer, but forgot the German words. I knew what he was asking me, however, and proceeded to explain the process without the technical terms. Amazingly, Strobl praised me for knowing enough about the theory that I could explain it without jargon. He gave me the highest grade possible.

The next day, I had another oral exam with Professor Hess. Professor Hess was the newest addition to the Psychology Institute, and it was her first university level teaching post. The exam with her was the opposite of the exam with Strobl the day before. Her questions focused on specific words or phrases she already had in mind. Rather than probe my grasp of the field, it seemed she wanted me to probe her mind.

Later, when I became an examiner, I understood Hess better. Because she didn't feel confident in the subject area, she needed my answers to fall within the narrow window of her knowledge. Her lack of confidence meant that my answers, beyond satisfying the exam criteria, had to ratify her knowledge, and ultimately her rank. Unlike Strobl, she couldn't follow my thinking on the topic. She needed it to conform to what she was thinking.

It sounds obvious, but a position of power—like every role—has tasks, duties, and responsibilities you are accountable for fulfilling. Obvious, sure, but power offers a plethora of options for hiding insecurity, incompetence, and taking shortcuts. In fact, the reason people so often misuse their rank is that the greater power you have and the greater your responsibilities, the less oversight you encounter. You have much more opportunity to use your role to protect your vulnerability (like Professor Hess), to shirk your duties, or to hide your incompetence.

The quickest way to undermine your legitimacy is to take advantage of that opportunity. Most of us are conscientious, but there are some unconscious ways in which we shirk our duties, without ever knowing we are doing so. What can you do to increase your awareness?

Don't fight your limits. Doing your job means knowing when you can't. No one is all-powerful. Responsibly fulfilling the duties of your role includes admitting your limitations—when you lack the energy, knowledge, or resources to perform or fulfill your duties. This requires an honest self-evaluation of your capacities, the humility to seek help, and the openness to vulnerability that allows you to refer the client or the job to someone else if appropriate, adjust and realign your priorities, or even step down if necessary.

To use your power well, honestly assess your capacity for power: ask for feedback, evaluate your performance, continue to learn, keep your skill level current, and seek out help when you feel you're in beyond your abilities.

A high-ranking role can easily become a curtain to hide behind. Like Professor Hess, whenever we feel insecure about our abilities, have trouble admitting we don't know something, or fear looking weak, we're at great risk. If someone asks a question and we don't know the answer, we can lie, change the subject, put another person on the spot, or even humiliate the one asking the question by criticizing it or them *ad hominem*.

Even when we can admit we don't know something, being in a high-ranking role becomes hypnotic over time. We come to believe we must soldier on, responsible for everyone else's well-being. We take on the responsibility for keeping everything going. Playing the hero is a temptation to watch out for. Your high-status role may be extraordinary but you are not. You have the same fears, needs, and limitations as the next person. And, by playing the hero, you're refusing to share the role. I've seen this play out in numerous ways. In particular, those in the helping professions are at risk of going beyond their limits to help others.

Years ago, I was called in to consult with a social work agency team. A client had lodged a complaint against them for boundary violations. They were being audited by the state regulatory agency, and they asked me to help them debrief the incident to learn as much as possible from it.

Nadia, a case worker, had counseled one of her clients, who was living in a domestic violence situation, to leave her partner. Believing the woman was at risk, Nadia thought she had done the right thing. Actually, she had overstepped her bounds. Instead of making the risk clear to her client and outlining the options she had to deal with the situation, Nadia told her what decision was "best." It may not seem like a big difference, and yet, in the role of social worker, Nadia's opinions came with authority. What she felt was a strong suggestion was experienced as meddling and, in fact, crossed a boundary.

Nadia's sense of justice overrode her professional concern. In the face of abuse, she lost sight of her limits. In this instance, she offended her client, but it could have been worse: she could have jeopardized the client's safety by encouraging her to leave.

While no one wants to be held back by their doubts, limits belong to the human condition. Not all fear is meant to be overcome. Remember the limbic states we discussed earlier? Fear is a primal emotion, and sometimes it is an early warning signal that we could die. Of course, sometimes we're meant to overcome fear, but not always. It's important to ask ourselves whether we need to push past our fear, or to recognize that the time may not be right to move forward.

Opening up to limits makes us sustainable leaders. Our fatigue may not mean we need coffee; maybe it's a signal that we need to come in the next day, after having rested, and finish the job. Opening up to limits means taking your limits and struggles seriously. We can't deplete all of our resources and burn ourselves out to singlehandedly keep things going. If we do, then we work beyond our capacity: our body starts to break down and we require more and more substances to stay awake. Over time, our thinking and energy diminish. In time, we make poor decisions, snap at people, forget important details, and lose our patience. Thus, acknowledging our lack of energy, resources, skill, or experience can be important for our well-being, and for the well-being of the whole as well.

Guard against the old guard. Being in a powerful role, any role, for a long time brings seniority. Even an informal role can create a sense of seniority, familiarity, and comfort. You become part of the "old guard" and it feels great. It's the feeling of deep organizational knowledge and mastery, of familiarity and family. And it often comes with a great deal of status and recognition.

But those in the old guard can unconsciously evade their duties. One's status is related to the status quo, so as a veteran you can find yourself defending your role by resisting change, feeling threatened by newcomers and rookies, and hoarding knowledge so as to make others dependent on you. You aren't helpful or welcoming, or may even ignore others' needs for orientation or support as they learn and adjust to their new roles in a new department or organization. After all, you've "paid your dues"—why shouldn't others be able to do the same?

I once had a client, Cassandra, who was exceptional at what she did. She was promoted and was thrilled to work for her new boss, Amir. He had a reputation for making things happen, and scoring big wins. Cassandra thought she lucked out when she was assigned to his team. Little did she know that seven years later, while all her friends had been promoted and had career-enhancing opportunities, she would still be there, working for her same boss. Amir never sent her on leadership courses, never let her make presentations to the leadership team, but had her do all the background research, for which he took all the credit. He never acknowledged her help. When Cassandra would ask about promotions and opportunities for advancement, Amir would shake his head and mention Cassandra's weaknesses and skill gaps.

One of the last things we ever consider, when dealing with someone who is in a position of power greater than ours, is that they could see us as a threat. But it happens. Teachers, supervisors, bosses, and even parents can feel threatened by and jealous of their students, subordinates, or children. It's doubly devastating because we're not simply treated poorly, but treated poorly by the very people whom we turn to for support. Instead of feeling proud of your progress, your mother finds a reason to dismiss it or minimize it, by comparing you to your sister who did better. You turn to your supervisor for help, and she questions your judgments and belittles your interventions. The people on whom you rely and trust betray you. It's a devastating realization: not only will they refuse to help you develop, but they will also use your vulnerability to keep you down, to protect their status.

As a member of the old guard, you can also fall into the trap of *over-expertise*. In a high-ranking role, especially one earned through mastery, you become a consultant. People frequently seek out your wisdom and counsel. Over time, you can get used it. It feels good to have people solicit your advice, ask for your opinions, appreciate your insights, and follow your guidance. But before you know it, you're dispensing advice to everyone—about everything. Your knowledge in one field becomes a license to act as an expert in every field. You come to believe your knowledge expands to all domains and disciplines, with equal validity.

Sometimes this happens to entrepreneurs. Having successfully created a business from scratch, and having managed all areas from the beginning, the entrepreneur has a hard time letting go. They're not only attached to the business, but also to their identity as founder, which can make them believe they fully apprehend all other areas of the business: finance, operation, marketing, or management. They struggle to let go of the reins and often fail when they insist on running their company alone.

There is a fine line between being a wise counselor with deep organizational knowledge and expertise, and being the old guard who jealously defends their tenure and seniority, overestimates their expertise, and dispenses advice inappropriately. It's tempting to rest on your laurels, enjoy the level of mastery you've attained, and not challenge yourself to learn more, increase your skills, or stay current.

The challenge for those with seniority is to keep learning, expose what they don't know, support newcomers, and be willing to share their expertise and knowledge by actively mentoring others to take over their role.

Doable Practice #8: Do Your Job and Know Your Limits

Look back over your day or your week, and note times when you felt you reached your energy limit, but pushed yourself to go on. It may have been a limit to your physical energy, or it could also have been a limit in terms of knowledge, capacity, or patience with something. Ask yourself two questions: What are you afraid would have happened, had you allowed yourself to stop? Think of three benefits you would have had if you had allowed yourself to stop or pause.

Guideline #9: Get Your Needs Met — Elsewhere

Dennis Kozlowski, the ex-CEO of Tyco International, was convicted of accepting $81 billion in illegal bonuses. He was notorious for his extravagance and obscene expenditures. He used company finances to pay for a $15,000 stand for dog umbrellas in his $30 million New York City apartment, along with $6,000 shower curtains. The final coup de grace was holding a fortieth birthday party for his wife, disguised as a shareholder meeting, for which Tyco paid $1 million. Held on the Italian island of Sardinia, the event famously featured an ice sculpture of Michelangelo's *David* urinating Stolichnaya vodka.

That's an extreme example, but it shows how easy it is to put self-interest ahead of the organization. Don't use your role for personal gain. Ever. This seems obvious, but we're human. We have longings, needs, and desires. Power avails us with easy access to fulfill them. It frequently happens without knowledge that we're doing it. The big, egregious exploitations—greedy grabs for power, sex, or more money—are easy to see. What's harder to perceive are the teeny slips and lapses, the ones that seem harmless at the time but lead us down the path to greater abuses of power: encouraging the fawning behavior of a student, asking our assistants to do personal errands, trying to get our child to take sides in a fight with our ex-spouse.

How can you guard against this?

Know your needs. Unless you know your needs, you won't know where and when you're tempted to satisfy them. We're all at risk: we all have a need for satisfying relationships, to feel good about ourselves, and to avoid pain. When you occupy a high-ranking role, or you have the admiration of students, clients, or employees, it's very difficult to become aware of your needs. There are so many people around you who need you and want your attention that unless you have an unerring devotion to your personal development, you will be tempted to satisfy your needs through the admiration of others.

Knowing your needs is the first step. The second is having methods and means to satisfy them. If you don't, you'll reach for the role to do it for you. This is a constant conflict of interest we need to fight against. Opening up to what's within—having needs, period—requires courage, self-awareness, and devotion to your continual growth. You must be committed to succeeding because it is an arduous effort and there are no alternatives.

Grow your personal life. In classical psychoanalytic training, trainees were not permitted to quit their jobs before they could work full-time as analysts, because their financial needs would interfere with their judgment. It was a classic conflict of interest: as analysts, they had to recommend treatment—how many times per week the client was to attend sessions. But as beginners without full-time employment, how would they be able to disentangle their financial interest from the equation? Keeping their day jobs while they grew their practice kept some of that financial strain out of the picture.

The proclivity to use your role for personal gain is just too great. The ease of using the role, combined with the difficulty of working on yourself, creates a massive conflict of interest. Rules and guidelines aren't enough. Commitment is a start, but you also need to set up structures for yourself to prevent abuse. You must be able to spend time growing your personal life.

Your high-ranking role needs to be relativized—put in proper scale—by something else of great importance: a family, relationship, spiritual or religious practice—something that gives you an enormous sense of purpose. Lacking else to fill a deep relational, spiritual, and emotional void, you will be tempted to use your role to fill it.

Your personal life is where you get your most intimate and personal needs met. If you have trouble at home, or lack friends, or have nowhere and no one else to help you fill your intimate and emotional needs, you will naturally be tempted to use your high-power role for this.

If you work in the financial service industry, or in an area with a lot of financial temptation, make sure your finances are in order. If you work as a therapist, teacher, or doctor, with young, vulnerable, or admiring clientele, make sure you have a satisfying, rich and intimate personal life. If you feel unfilled spiritually, seek out a spiritual practice or religious affiliation that puts meaning and purpose in your life.

And there's another reason for growing your personal life. Leading is hard work. You need the love, support, and sanctity of a rich and rewarding personal life, friends and family, loved ones and meaningful activities to sustain you. Just as one person in your life cannot fulfill all your needs, neither can a role.

Doable Practice #9: Get Your Needs Met — Elsewhere

Take an inventory of the things that you get from your high-ranking role that feel rewarding, satisfying, and that you would miss if you didn't have. What are they? Appreciate them! Ask yourself, "Can I find these elsewhere? If I had to give up this role, where and how else could I obtain these satisfying experiences?"

These steps for making your power legitimate help you gain the respect of others. And with their respect comes your legitimacy. Your power has to be ratified by the others, and this can only happen through behavior worth following.

But you do not lead in a vacuum. You occupy a role of power within a context and a culture. The next set of power guidelines concerns the culture and context around you. Our behavior might be impeccable, but we are surrounded by the perks, privileges, and temptations of opportunity. The last set of rules helps us mitigate opportunity, reduce the temptations for personal gain that power offers, and create healthy places of power.

7

Share Your Personal Power

Power ought to serve as a check to power.
—CHARLES DE SECONDAT

I am not interested in power for power's sake,
but I'm interested in power that is moral,
that is right and that is good.
—MARTIN LUTHER KING, JR.

The old saying, "opportunity makes the thief" is nowhere more true than when it comes to power. Power provides us with ample opportunities to take advantage of our role. We have control over others, access to money, privileged information, along with reduced oversight and supervision. In addition to the tangible assets we have, we also have psychological influences such as disinhibition, more freedom to act, a greater belief in our own ideas, and less interest in others' feedback.

These opportunities create a constant conflict of interest: on the one hand, our job is to serve the interests of our clients, students, or organizations; on the other, we're tempted with numerous and immediate opportunities to enrich ourselves at the expense of others. When it comes to opportunity, self-awareness alone doesn't cut it. No matter how valiantly we try to be conscious of our behaviors and ethical in our actions, we aren't very good at monitoring ourselves.

It's not for lack of will, or due to weak moral fiber. It's because conflict of interest creates an unconscious bias that changes how we analyze a situation. If, as a teacher, I have two papers to grade, and one is from a student who openly admires and flatters me, while the other is from a student who's been challenging and difficult all semester, my feelings, even if I'm assiduously trying to be impartial, will color what I read.

Self-interest causes blind spots; even if we are aware of what we're doing, we create stories and theories that cast our behavior in a more favorable light. Jonathan Haidt, moral psychologist, calls it the "emotional dog wagging its rational tail."[1] Many of our judgments, ideas, and beliefs are first formed by an intuitive, unconscious reaction or emotion. We then create rational arguments to defend the limbic response, unaware that it is "just a feeling." Our emotions drive the bus, or in Haidt's words, wag the tail.

Let's say, however, we're able to be hyper-conscientious and highly aware of ourselves, and we manage to control our self-interest. It can happen. You can curb some cravings sometimes, right? But then there's the second pesky problem: other people. We're influenced by other people, and by culture, in opaque, hard-to-notice ways. Like the proverbial frog in boiling water, we don't realize what's happened until we've been cooked through with cultural norms and values, aligned with the attitudes and beliefs of our organizational philosophy. Context shapes our behavior by shaping our understanding of right and wrong, good and bad.

Research demonstrates that social norms play a more profound role in our behavior than previously thought. A large-scale, thirty-year study of obesity using social mapping found that a person's chances of becoming obese increased by 57% if they had a friend who became obese over a shared period of time.[2] Studies related to ethical behavior and social norms resulted in similar findings: for instance, the more exposure someone has to others' unethical activity, the greater the chances the subject will themselves behave unethically. The people in your community play a greater role in your decision-making than any other factor.[3] In other words, even if we are honest, law-abiding, and conscientious citizens, if we spend enough time in a given culture, we will come to view our behavior through the lens of that culture's norms. When "everyone is doing it," then every person does indeed do it.

While context gives us opportunity to deviate, not all contexts are equal in their influence. The possibility for misusing our power is highest in those contexts in which temptations are high, oversight is low, the perpetrator and victim both have a degree of anonymity, and the culture permits some infractions.

Think of the financial services industry. For bankers and financial advisors who work alone most of the time, the temptation for misconduct is enormous, and the culture within the industry has a tendency to "permit" or at least be lax about indiscretions. Additionally, the client may be unknown—perhaps a faceless corporation or a number on a spreadsheet—or at least the so-called crime doesn't occur face-to-face. To top it off, the overseeing body is comprised of former banking executives and advisors, i.e., present and former colleagues.

Some industries share these characteristics, and thus are most prone to abuse. In fact, seven of the twelve least ethical multinationals, as quantified by the research firm Covalence, were mining or oil and gas companies.[4] Two were agricultural chemical companies.

Organizations, not just people, have their self-interests, which they dedicate vast resources to protecting. Examples of organizational decisions that prioritize self-interest above others' considerations are plentiful.

The Catholic Church has protected itself by denying decades of sexual abuse and simply reassigning repeat sexual offenders to different positions, rather than removing them outright—and thereby protecting children.

NASA's high-level managers, under pressure to retain federal funding and stick to their launch deadline, ignored engineers' warnings of structural defects on the Challenger Space Shuttle and proceeded with the scheduled launch, which resulted in the deaths of seven people.

Discovering evidence that assistant football coach Jerry Sandusky had sexually assaulted underage boys on university property, the leadership at Pennsylvania State University ignored and attempted to cover up the incidents, allowing Sandusky to assault children for fourteen more years until one of the victims came forward. A court eventually found him guilty of forty-five counts of child sexual abuse.

Car manufacturers have historically suppressed knowledge of faulty parts, determining that the cost of recall and bad publicity was worth the risk of a few lawsuits.

We could say the leaders at the top of these organizations were sociopaths, or we could fault the organizations for lax regulations. But either explanation overlooks the fact that this tendency can and does happen everywhere. A bright organizational identity casts a long shadow. Organizational norms, joined with a powerful self-interest, compromise decision-making.

Self-awareness isn't enough. All of these factors—an individual's self-interest, the organization's need to protect itself, the leadership's post-hoc rationalization that passes for judgment, the influence of others on one's decision-making, and the temptations of and easy access to opportunity—make it plain to see why rules and ethical guidelines can at least partially mitigate conflicts of interest.

Laws and guidelines improve accountability, restrict access to assets or currency, and limit the scope of each individual's position, all in order to reduce conflict of interest. But while we can constrain opportunity, we cannot completely control it. Most laws that limit opportunity are enacted after the fact. As the adage goes: it's like putting up the fence after the horse has bolted. When opportunity knocks, when perks and privileges tempt us, no rule or guideline can stand in our way.

Don't misunderstand: we *need* rules, but also, as we saw in the last chapter, knowledge of our liabilities. Understanding where our needs tempt us and taking steps to get those needs met are two ways of preventing ourselves from misusing our roles. Additionally, we also need organizational habits hardwired into our processes to help reduce bias, unconscious self-interest, and organization-wide blind spots. Instead of relying on willpower, self-awareness, or even feedback, creating habits—repeated actions—that become automatic behaviors are useful for things that carry great temptation. When we're tempted, our judgment is clouded, and we're unable to rely on our compromised awareness. It's at that moment that it's useful for an automatic behavior to kick in and allow us to see things, and behave in ways outside our self-interested frames of reference.

The last set of power laws—or guidelines—offer five behaviors, habits, and attitudes that individuals can adopt (even if their organizations don't) to help limit opportunity and make each organization and team a place of positive and healthy power.

Guideline #10: Shake Up Your Cognitive Egg[5]

The higher you travel on the organizational ladder, the further your grasp on reality loosens. Remember the "death zone" of power? You no longer receive immediate feedback about your actions, nor do you experience the consequences of your decisions and actions as others do. You live in a bubble, surrounded by others who have a personal stake in your powerful role. They may be afraid of your authority, or dependent on you for their livelihood. Being associated with you enhances their career success, and they may be emotionally dependent on your love and attention.

When everyone in your bubble affirms your high-ranking role, you can no longer see yourself clearly or evaluate yourself and your effectiveness. Moreover, it's easy to fall prey to self-confirming beliefs

and judgments that further your self-interest. Humans and organizations are prone to *confirmation bias*: we choose information that
confirms what we already think and ignore that which doesn't. Even
lacking power, humans are notorious for believing what they want
to believe, facts be damned. It's virtually impossible for information
contrary to what we want to believe to make it through the firewall
of our ego and its self-serving theories.

Positional power makes it a serious danger. When those around
you are afraid to challenge you, you can cherry-pick the feedback
that confirms your beliefs. Your high-power position shields you
from social contexts outside your influence, further limiting the
opportunity to grow beyond what you already know. You "buy your
own pitch."

Confirmation bias is tricky. Even when we think we're open to
feedback, we often interpret it through the filter of our cultural
beliefs, make it fit to the point of only slight discomfort. Or we
minimize or disregard it, or we discredit the messenger. One example of confirmation bias, for instance, is attributing the low
number of women and minorities in leadership roles to their lack of
skill or to biological inferiority. Another is a therapist who calls
clients "resistant" when they don't follow his interventions, or a
teacher or school counselor who calls children "defiant" or "opposi-
tional" when they disrupt and don't pay attention.

Organizations are prone to this confirmation bias, and the
stronger the organizational identity, the more institutionalized its
bias is. Whistleblowers are routinely disregarded as people who
"couldn't cut it," didn't "fit in," or were in some way substandard.
When organizations conduct secretive internal investigations not
subject to independent review, it is a case of confirmation bias: they
believe in their capacity to police themselves, without bias. The
Pentagon, for instance, believes the military should be in charge of
investigating and prosecuting sexual assault within the military—
through its own chain of command—even though a large percentage

of sexual assaults reported are committed by members of the victim's chain of command.[6]

We frequently police the conflict of interests described here through methods such as audits and external, regulatory oversight. While these methods are both valuable and necessary, they aren't sufficient on their own. We can still comply with regulations while refusing to embrace them as a core value. Conformity and obedience may change our behaviors, but not necessarily our beliefs or underlying biases.

We need a more robust solution still. We need something that forces us to think about our worlds in a fundamentally different way. To stay aware of ourselves, to catch our confirmation biases, we need to challenge our basic assumptions, beliefs, and perceptions of ourselves and of others. We need to be confronted by dissonant data through rigorous methods that shake up our "cognitive egg." This includes building in *double-loop learning* and *opening up talk*.

Build in double-loop learning. Organizational psychologist Chris Argyris defined two types of learning: "single-loop" and "double-loop" learning.[7] Single-loop learning is self-reflection based on one's own principles, theories or values. An organization using single-loop learning will modify its behavior—but only within the narrow confines of its own values and assumptions. Many performance management systems, for instance, solicit questions about effectiveness, performance, competencies, and the like. But the information the systems gather reflects only the values and beliefs of the organization using it. The ostensible answer usually involves doing more or less of something, of making adjustments to what's already in place. Feedback that questions the organization's underlying assumptions usually isn't sought or accepted.

Double-loop learning, in contrast, exposes the organizational knowledge base. It illuminates the assumptions, values, and belief matrix inherent in the system itself and is therefore better at breaking down the firewall that keeps feedback out. Double-loop learning means that not only can an organization analyze and reflect on its own behavior and action—it can also question its underlying values and beliefs.

Many years ago I worked with a teacher, Jodie. She was an exceptional educator, and her students were motivated, eager, and happy to come to school. By all accounts, she was a superstar. But one day she came to me and complained her school was in trouble over funding. Though the students were highly engaged and doing well, it seemed they only performed average or below average on standardized tests. Some of her students' reading and math scores fell below the state average. How can this be? Jodie wondered.

I asked her about the state tests, and she scoffed.

"Teaching to the test trains students to learn how to answer test questions," she said. "They don't teach children to think, they don't inspire a love of learning, and they don't help them apply knowledge from the classroom in real-life situations."

It was great point. Jodie may be right, but her beliefs weren't the issue. Although she had a valid position, she was using single-loop learning, and discrediting other forms of measurement and feedback. She didn't permit herself or her class to absorb methods past the firewall of her own educational theories. She didn't want to engage with assessment that came from a point of view she disagreed with.

Jodie's problem isn't about failing to teach her students. It's thinking her standards are the only ones that matter. Whether testing "works" or not, the point is that test scores are data that her school must consider. By engaging with, rather than ignoring that data, she would allow herself to be challenged and extend her thinking outside her belief system.

Ram Charan, one of the leading management consultants in the world, helps CEOs make better decisions. He understands how critical it is for leaders to be able to challenge their assumptions.

Charan gives an example of double-loop learning in which the leadership of a company invites outsiders into its board's strategy sessions to critique and challenge the leaders' thinking and shed light on hidden assumptions they could otherwise be missing. He helped one of his clients, a CEO, challenge his own and his company's assumptions by meeting...

> ...four times a year with about four other CEOs of large but noncompeting, diverse global companies. They examine the world from multiple angles, looking for unstoppable trends, and share their best thinking about how each could play out. Then this CEO goes back to his own weekly management meetings and throws out a bunch of hand grenades to shake up people's thinking.[8]

We don't need to be CEOs to do this. We don't have to be anyone special to challenge our organizational assumptions.

A colleague of mine who works as vice president of marketing at a mid-sized personal care products company told me about the organization's new business-building strategy. One of the main criteria was that any new idea had to come from outside the scope of everyday business. By preventing themselves from revisiting the same concepts and customer opportunities they had discussed in the past, the company began to think differently about what they could accomplish. They ventured outside of their old, predictable ways of analyzing the situation.

Their big breakthrough came when they began to speak differently about the company and its growth strategy to vendors, customers, and other potential partners. It was incredibly energizing for the executive and sales team and altered the team's culture. The company's strategy has allowed them to break into a previously off-limits sales channel and eventually resulted in a large leap in revenue growth.

Open up talk. Another way to challenge your assumptions is by connecting with people in your organization, at all levels, to hear feedback, and solicit and engage with all the news—bad and good. Great
leaders open themselves up to feedback and criticism. They allow
for methods for people to give input without fear of consequence.
They speak to people on the others' own turf: by leaving their offices or setting up forums and methods for people to speak their
minds. They conduct exit interviews, receiving frank feedback from
people who left about why they left and what was problematic or
difficult for them in their jobs. They talk to people "on the front
lines" those who most critically engage with customers, customer
service issues, complaints, or other kinds of problems that aren't
immediately visible to management.

One of the most creative applications of this idea comes from a
colleague who worked with male juvenile offenders in a mental
health facility. Once a month, he had an "open forum" where the
youth and the staff could come together and talk about the issues on
their mind. Oftentimes some of the young men were angry or upset
at the staff, or complained about the strictness of some of the rules.
It wasn't an opportunity to change policy, but the ability to speak
openly about the things that bothered them had a terrific effect on
the culture. It also created an easier connection between the youth
and the staff, carrying over into their everyday interactions.

To open up talk, you must first establish a culture in which
difficult, uncomfortable things can be aired, discussed openly, and
acted upon. My colleague spent many months discussing this idea
with people in the hospital, and doing it in small ways, before imple-
menting it. Every organization has its "undiscussables"—topics that
are awkward to raise, issues and problems that are gossiped about, the
"elephant in the room" that everyone knows but no one discusses.[9]
Often, undiscussables have to do with power dynamics, relationship
disputes, and conflict over difference of social identity, working habits, or communication style, compounded by organizational norms

that feel constricting and oppressive. Undiscussables make teamwork difficult, disturb relationships, and create toxic atmospheres. But they also contain valuable information about the organization's identity.

Instituting a time and place to discuss undiscussables is one healthy way to monitor the organization's confirmation bias. By holding regularly scheduled open forums or meetings where difficult topics can be put on the table, discussed openly, and worked through without fear of reprisals, we see what we've missed.

But the presence of power inhibits people to talk freely and openly. Even with enlightened leadership, one with the best of intentions to listen to feedback, it's still necessary to implement anonymous comment-gathering methods. And even if people trust the leadership, they still run additional risks: falling afoul of co-workers, or being labeled as a troublemaker for bringing up unpleasant topics.

Both methods are important: we need opportunities to discuss in the open and we also need anonymous comments and feedback. One without the other won't work. An open culture that lacks the mechanism for anonymous feedback creates only a partially open climate, one that is open to those things that are safe to mention but not those that remain hidden for fear of reprisal. A culture with only anonymous feedback but no opportunity for open discussion will promote secrecy and indirectness, creating an atmosphere of mistrust, and undermining teamwork and camaraderie.

Doable Practice #10: Shake Up Your Cognitive Egg

Create your own personal advising group, a "board of directors" comprised of friends, colleagues, and peers outside your profession, industry, group, or department. Deliberately seek people who have different methods, backgrounds, and frameworks than yours. Set up monthly meetings, and ask for advice and input—not on the pressing problems you need help with, but on those things you feel most confident about.

You may not agree, or like what the board has to say, but engage with their input, and see what you learn from it. Were there pieces of advice that surprised you? How has their input "shaken up your cognitive egg"? What can you bring into your role or organization?

Guideline #11: Don't Measure Yourself with Your Own Yardstick

To catch our confirmation biases, we need to evaluate ourselves in diverse ways, not just according to the values we deem important.

In the United States, two million people admitted to a hospital get an infection they didn't have before because a staff person did not wash their hands.[10] In spite of some of the best medical training in the world, and state-of-the-art facilities, medical errors are the third largest cause of death in the United States, with between 210,000 and 440,000 patients each year suffering some form of preventable harm that contributes to their death.[11]

The surgeon, writer, and health care reform advocate Atul Gawande observed that the hospitals' means for correcting the problem routinely failed to solve it. So he did something radical. He looked for a solution entirely outside the discipline of medicine. He found two other industries that dealt with extremely complex processes and had a high fatality risk: aviation and skyscraper construction. Though similar in that regard, they differed in another: their fatality rates were dramatically lower.

What did these industries do differently? What kind of method or technology did they employ? They used a checklist. These industries controlled the fatality rate by compelling their teams to use checklists: low-tech, inexpensive, old-school checklists. Gawande attempted to implement the same method across hospitals in the

United States. His results? The hospitals in the test group that used the checklist saw their death rates fall by 47%.

But there's a twist: In spite of those remarkable results, hospitals resisted making the change. Two years after Gawande wrote about his findings in *The New Yorker*, less than 20% of the hospitals in the United States had adopted it.[12] Even Gawande himself resisted using it. He admitted that he adopted it at Harvard, where he works, only because he didn't want to appear hypocritical.[13]

Why would something so inexpensive, so easy to create, and so successful—at saving lives, mind you—not immediately show up in every hospital around the world? Because of cultural resistance. The checklist method challenged a sacred hospital tradition: hierarchy. By giving everyone on the team the power to check on each other's preparedness, the method effectively put every team member on equal par—nurses and surgeons alike. This just wasn't how things had been done in the medical profession, ever.

The hospitals in this case didn't only disregard a new method, which many organizations do when a proposed change runs contrary to their implicit norms; they also discredited the *value* of the data. Hospital-created infections, alarming as the rate was, did not cause alarms. The hospitals either didn't include infections as a measurement of success or failure, or, if they did, they minimized their prominence.

As a patient, that seems atrocious. But think about it in terms of your profession: What are the benchmarks for measuring a coach's success? Or a facilitator's? A teacher's? A therapist's? Or a manager's? A parent's? We might be surprised to see how many fields use their ingrained yardsticks to measure success. When a profession or industry creates its own measurement and evaluation system, it tends to choose those qualities in its field of vision, while leaving out others that are of greater importance to its clients and customers.

When we measure our progress and evaluate our work using our own yardsticks, we inevitably wind up giving ourselves high marks.

It's just too easy to pick and choose the kind of feedback we want and the methods through which we want to get it. We all have an inclination to prefer measuring ourselves on standards of our preference.

As a trainer, I found out I had a bias towards questions on my feedback forms that ask participants about facilitation style, participant engagement, the experiential nature of the learning activities, and clarity of presentation. What do these qualities have in common? They are my strengths. Was it conscious? Of course not. But when I sat down to write up the questions, those items came to mind first because they are most important to *me*. What about the organization of my written material? What about the quality of my visual presentation? What about the learning's ongoing relevance in the workplace? Should I have provided further reading and references? How easy was it for participants to translate the learning into their day-to-day personal and professional existences? These questions didn't come to me initially. They measure things I didn't value as much—not consciously, at least. They just weren't on my radar.

Instead, the feedback I solicited supported what I already valued, and hence, already did well. I tended to get high marks, of course—a classic self-fulfilling prophecy. And here's another wrinkle: as long as my courses were filled by participants who self-selected, the more my measuring system was validated. It was only when I began to work in organizational contexts where people did not self-select that I began to open up to different, and more challenging, benchmarks. It meant I had to see more critical feedback, but it also meant my teaching considerably improved. I began to use more visual aids, created more activities that engaged different forms of learning, and most importantly, designed activities and resources that helped participants connect learning to their workplaces and personal lives more directly and meaningfully.

It's important to question our own ways of measuring success and failure because power protects us from the results of our own actions. We're too far upstream to see or feel the results of our decisions as they flow downstream. Economic theory called this a *moral hazard*—a situation where the person or people making the decision don't suffer the consequences of the decision if it goes wrong. Instead, someone else—almost always someone with lower rank—bears the cost of the high-ranking individual's decision.[14]

If a student fails, it's a moral hazard if the teacher, school, or district doesn't face some consequences as well. If a company's wages are frozen, but its stock prices go up, a moral hazard has occurred. When a company outsources its manufacturing to another country and doesn't do its due diligence in researching the contractors hired, it has spawned a moral hazard. When a counselor or doctor gets paid a uniform salary, regardless of whether clients or patients improve, the conditions for a moral hazard are in place. Quota systems that reward or penalize officers based on the number of tickets or arrests they make sets up not only a moral hazard, but also the conditions for illegal abuse of power.

Measuring our success with our own set of criteria just won't do. We need to consider the values and needs of our customers, students, clients, and subordinates—and not just the things we, in a position of power, deem important. Additionally, like Gawande, we need to look outside our industry or discipline to see how others measure and assess progress. How do other industries, and disciplines measure themselves, seek feedback, engage in self-improvement, and solve their problems?

To close the gap between upstream and downstream, you must build in some accountability for your decision-making. Make sure that you, in some way, bear the cost and benefit of your actions.

Doable Practice #11: Don't Measure Yourself with Your Own Yardstick

Whether or not you have a formal evaluation system for your job or role, write down the criteria that you or others use to evaluate you, whether you parent, preach, coach, or lead.

Now, write down a second list of the criteria you *don't* use to evaluate yourself, no matter how far-fetched it may seem. That list should include things you value, but don't measure yourself with, as well as things you don't (yet) value. See if you can incorporate some, or even all of them into your feedback process, whatever it may be.

Guideline #12: Make the Rules of the Game Transparent

My Australian friend Anna once told me a story about the time her Indian teacher, Rani, visited her in Australia. Anna was hosting, and when Rani arrived, Anna showed her the kitchen, opening up cupboards and the refrigerator, giving her a tour of the food, pots and pans, plates, and cutlery.

"Please, make yourself at home," she said, thinking herself gracious.

Three days later, a few of Anna's friends came over and remarked that Rani had hardly been seen. "Have you even seen her eat?" one of them asked Anna. "Has she cooked anything?" Anna thought about it, and suddenly realized that Rani had, in fact, stayed in her room almost the entire time, hardly venturing outside at all, let alone cooking or eating a meal. Anna's friends were aghast, and scolded her for her poor hosting.

"Make yourself at home" sounds well-meaning, but it's not a great "game rule." Its meaning doesn't translate across differences of culture or rank. In India, custom dictates hosts serve their guests; few people native to the culture would expect guests to open up the host's refrigerator or cupboards and start cooking food for themselves.

When people don't know or can't follow the game rules, they can't play. That's why newcomers in a team or group often hang back. When you're new to a group or team, you don't know what's expected of you. You don't know what you are permitted to say, what nets you praise and what gets you in trouble. Those who set the game rules and those who know them have home-court advantage.

Proper use of power means taking care to make sure others are as informed as you are, so that they can participate to their fullest. To do this, *make your power transparent*, and *make the process rational*.

Be transparent about your authority. For people to engage and participate, they need to know who's in charge, how decisions get made, what's allowed and not allowed, and if there are means for disagreement or appeal.

Whether you are a teacher, parent, boss or mentor, you need to be clear and honest about your authority. When the underlying methodology and ideology of decision-making and reward aren't explicit, they will be perceived as arbitrary. When parents make arbitrary rules, children never know whether or not they can do something; it's a chaotic and emotionally unstable condition. When the boss sometimes stands by a rule, and then other times breaks or doesn't enforce it, he creates confusion and disorder. When a teacher conceals the basis of her grading system from students, students don't know what they're meant to learn, nor what skills the person at the head of the class is grading them on.

Whenever authority and rules are hidden, arbitrary, or just poorly explained, we create an individualist atmosphere, an atmosphere of competition and complicated and divisive rank dynamics. Some people get favored, others don't. Some participants understand the activity and can participate; others don't and appear less engaged. Some teachers hand out As while students in other classrooms where the same course is taught are lucky to get Cs. Some employees get promotions, others don't, all without a clear method people can make use of. Whenever the rules for participation, promotion, advancement, or success are unclear, people suspect special favors or unfair treatment is at play.

A shared knowledge of the rules of the game enables everyone to participate. When the teacher tells the students on what basis she grades papers, everyone knows what to focus on. When the lecturer or meeting chair clarifies whether questions are permitted or not, she's clarifying how the audience should participate. When a dad explains to his daughter that she isn't allowed to go to her friend's house because he doesn't feel she'll be safe, he's showing her that he bases his rules on reasons. His rules are therefore subject to debate, and if not debate, then discussion at least.

Transparency entails being upfront about your expectations, rules, and standards. It means making available the means for disagreement, rebuttal, and dissent. It gives the other person freedom and choice. This is especially important whenever our role gives us specialized knowledge the client lacks. A coach should explain to her client how she works, what her modus operandi and expectations are, and what the client can expect. Then, the client can decide to agree to those terms or not. When the therapist makes it clear that her opinions can be discussed and debated, the client can fully engage in the process. But when the therapist doesn't, or when she frames the client's feedback in psychological argot, she's hiding her authority in her own method.

Sure, it's well-intentioned, but an attempt to stand on equal footing can backfire. If you have the power to hire, terminate, evaluate, pass, or fail someone you work with, you're not equal to them. If you make more money, or have different rights or levels of access to resources, you are not the same.

Make your power transparent. Overt power is dangerous, but hidden power is really scary.

Years ago, early on in my career, I examined a student who was older than me, and had more clinical experience. Though I had deeper knowledge of the method, I felt nervous due to her experience. I imagined she resented being examined by someone younger, with less professional maturity. So I felt insecure about my role as examiner.

When she first entered my office, I chatted with her in a friendly, collegial way. I was trying to put myself at ease, but also—perhaps unconsciously—disarm her in case she did feel resentful. It was a major mistake. Within a few minutes, I realized there were gaps in her knowledge, and I sat in the awkward position of having to give difficult feedback after having acted so affable. When I delivered the feedback, I completely overcompensated, merely spitting out the facts so I could get over my nervousness quickly. No doubt I came across as officious and stern—a complete turnaround from my previous behavior. The exam was a failure. It was *my* failure. I dropped my rank, acted collegial, and then hit her with a thunderbolt. Rather than be transparent with my rank from the beginning, I minimized it out of my own insecurity.

In retrospect, I should have first challenged my own sense of insecurity. I either should not have examined her if I truly wasn't up for it, or I should have encouraged myself to identify with my knowledge, what legitimized me in that role of examiner. Second, my attempt to put myself at ease was wrong. I should have put myself at ease *before* the exam, and not embroil her in my need to calm my nerves. Finally, when delivering the feedback, I could have been more honest about being nervous. Rather than try to suppress it, I could have sat with my own discomfort.

Make the process rational, not just relational. Make processes for participation rational. While transparency ensures the rules are known, discussed, and available to all, rational provides a process that can be followed. A consistent and regular process does not hinge on relationship, whim, or bias. It is equitable.

When you say, "my door is always open," you're not being equitable; not everyone feels free to knock on your door and interrupt you. To do so would require some relational ability, social boldness, or familiarity with you and your style. So while the attitude is transparent, it's not rational.

Many groups I work with value egalitarianism, collaboration, and shared power. Rather than abide by concrete rules or guidelines, people are encouraged instead to bring up issues directly with each other. This approach is a double-edged sword. While it fosters collaborative and egalitarian behavior, in practice it is sometimes experienced as inequitable because not everyone shares the feeling of belonging, or has the social skills, extraversion, or courage to speak up. Not everyone is equally prepared or equipped to have frank conversations, nor to advocate for themselves. Women, on average, are known to be less likely to negotiate salary increases, believing instead that the boss will initiate the conversation. Introverts will more likely avoid direct engagement with others. And speaking up in public favors some cultures, while it disadvantages others. We don't need to make rules for every social interaction, but it's important to understand how individuals can feel relational methods to be preferential and exclusionary.

Doable Practice #12: Make the Rules of the Game Transparent
Make an inventory answering the following questions: What are the ways other people give you feedback? Do people know how they can give you feedback? Are the processes regular and scheduled into your calendar? Are they known by all, and published somewhere? Are newcomers briefed on these processes? Do the methods for feedback require people to use certain skills or abilities, and is it equitable—is everyone equally versed in those abilities?

Look over your answers. How transparent are your methods for giving feedback? What are some ways your methods can be improved?

Guideline #13: Cultivate Role Conflict

During the 2012 U.S. presidential campaign, Mitt Romney gave an interview on ABC's *Good Morning America*, wherein he defined annual middle-class income as ranging from $200,000 to $250,000.[15] How close was Romney's estimate? Median household income for that year, according to census data, was about \$53,000. (Romney's income in 2011, by the way, was \$13.7 million.)

As Romney's gaffe shows, when you're in a high-status role, or a position of privilege and power, it's easy to fall out of touch. We get to decide what world we live in. Everywhere we go, everyone we talk to, and everything we do occurs within that world, confirming our view of life and, equally, verifying our rank. We become a member of an elite club, a VIP surrounded by like-minded subordinates and sycophants.

Remember the danger we discussed in Chapter 1, the lack of role conflict? It's good for our psychological and social health to occupy many roles, each with different ranks. The higher your rank, the more important it is to engage in activities, fulfill responsibilities, and have areas of your life in which you don't hold power, where no one knows or cares about your other, supposedly important role.

Very high-power individuals have to contend with this daily. Some do it better than others. The cult of celebrity for high-power individuals can trap them into their high-status identity *exclusively*. They have followers and staff, or an entourage, a small group of people who reinforce and reflect back to them only their high-status identity. They check into hotels under assumed names and enter through the service door to avoid the public. They never have to sit in the doctor's waiting room, or drive around for hours, looking for parking. They don't have to stand for forty minutes in the checkout line behind a full carriage and a screaming baby. In fact, they don't have to wait in lines, period. Ever. Everywhere they go, the trappings of power come with them. They are released from the drudgery and frustration of everyday life.

Yet role conflict protects us against inflation and arrogance. It also reduces the addiction to power. Our high status has such profound benefit that we develop a deep-seated motive to keep it at all costs. But there are ways to protect ourselves. Like actors who choose to live outside of Hollywood's insular world, some high-power individuals choose to exist in their fullness, to not be constrained by their single, high-profile role.

Be a beginner somewhere. One truly helpful way to cultivate role conflict is to be a beginner. Learn something new. Put yourself in a position of uncertainty. Work at something you're bad at. Whatever you undertake, deliberately hunt out opportunities to live outside the context in which your rank is reinforced. For some people, novice comes through personal relationships. Maintaining an intimate partnership is a humbling experience. So is raising children. For others, it might be learning the violin, or practicing judo. Every position of power is upheld by its context. And while it won't solve all the problems of power abuse, the task of learning about oneself outside that reinforcing context ought to be a requirement for all leaders.

Be a nobody. Anonymity is vital. Place yourself in a context where no one knows you, or where they don't care about your role—what you represent. When people relate to your role, they confirm your high rank. When no one knows who you are, you will be ranked according to the values of that context. Your rank will depend on elements outside your area of mastery, and outside your control. Those around you will accept you on the basis of things that have nothing to do with your fame, mastery, or expertise. This forces you to think about other aspects of your personality, and to get along with people outside your usual comfort zone. Importantly, you will have to rely on your social skills to gain respect, and not just your role.

Good leaders also learn how to "be nobody" in the midst of being a somebody. While one option is to have times and places in life where you can let go and step out of your role, good leaders also bring their "nobodiness" *into* their leadership role, by letting others have the spotlight, encouraging others to lead, giving credit to others, being humble and modest, and placing their interests in the service of something greater.

Doable Practice #13: Cultivate Role Conflict

Look over your current life, and activities. Do you see a mix of roles and rank? Where do you have high rank, and where are you a rookie, or at least not the most high-ranking person in the room? How could you achieve better balance?

Guideline #14: Fulfill the Noble Goal of Your Role

This is not a habit, but a belief—a mindset, something to strive for, and something that keeps your attention on the lofty goal behind your role. Beyond their demands and responsibilities, roles also have a function, a higher purpose at their core. As we saw in Chapter 6, a role is also an archetype, something universal. Part of that archetype is the principle or ideal behind the role. I call this the "noble goal" of your role.

Doctors live by the credo "First, Do No Harm." The teacher's credo is that all students can learn. The higher purpose of the therapeutic profession might be to serve the client's interest. The higher purpose or principle governing a CEO would be to further the company's mission, and further the interests of the stakeholders: employees, shareholders, customers, and in many cases, the public.

Not every profession has a credo, but it should. If you occupy a powerful role, find out what your personal and professional credo is: what higher principles guide your behavior and actions. To use power ethically and responsibly, you have to find the credo, the role's noble goal, and live by it. Let it guide you, and let it help you keep your eyes on the bigger goal—what the role demands of you.[16]

There are many times in a high-ranking role when you just don't know what to do. Ask yourself, "What does the role require of me?" That's one surefire way to check in with the noble goal. The question helps us raise our gaze above our limits, edges, fears, and petty interests. If you're afraid to have a conversation, uncertain about a direction, or having trouble discerning your own self-interest from the organization's needs, ask yourself: What does the role need me to do? What does this context demand?

This line of questioning becomes helpful when the task is hard, the temptation massive, or when you're up against a serious challenge. I remember when I first became an examiner in a graduate program that the challenge of having to fail someone felt insurmountable. When I learned, however, to use the higher purpose of teaching—to promote learning—as a way to fail someone, it helped me with that onerous task. Even the act of failing someone had to be done in a way that promoted and supported their learning. I have coached leaders who feel the same way about having to fire an employee. Serving the role, serving the larger needs of the organization, and serving the employee's interests allows us to step up and do difficult things in the best way possible with authenticity and purpose.

Years ago, I worked with the local police force on designing a crisis intervention and response training. One of the officers, Monique, a field training officer who mentored new recruits, told me the story of Roger, a new recruit to whom she was assigned. Monique clearly loved her job. I loved working with her because she had such passion and commitment to what she did. Even though she could have taken an easier role, she chose to be a field training officer because she loved teaching others, and she also just loved patrolling the neighborhoods, especially the ones she had grown up in. She knew every shopkeeper and their families. And she knew the kids on the street by name.

Roger was good, Monique said. He was smart, and had good instincts, but something about him bothered her. He was always checking emails and texting when they weren't patrolling. One thing in particular bothered Monique. When a call came over the radio, Roger would type in the address on the GPS. This exasperated

Monique. "This is your beat," she'd say. "You have to know it. You can't just follow directions on the screen."

Another thing that bothered her was Roger's lack of interest in people. Monique would also take a few extra minutes, chat with the guy behind the counter, or the little kid at the counter, and even though it was old-fashioned, she still handed out "junior officer badge" stickers to the kids. But Roger would walk off, and wait in the squad car until she finished, uninterested and impatient and checking his emails. But what really concerned her was his willingness to accept free coffee at cafes. Monique was strict about that and always insisted on paying. But Roger had no compunctions about taking the offer. It was awkward when she refused and he said, "Yeah, sure, thanks."

Monique said to me that she understood where he was coming from. She'd been on the force for twenty years, while he was getting an entry level salary, and raising two kids as the sole income earner. But what struck me was what Monique said about him next. "It's just a job for him, I'm afraid," she said. "It could be any job, and that's the problem."

Monique meant that he wasn't in touch with the noble goal of the role. His personal interests were stronger than his sense of duty. He didn't misuse his power, but it was a sloppy use of power. He wasn't relating to the larger set of responsibilities, of what it meant to be an officer. In fact, Roger identified more with being 'entry level' than with being the 'police officer.' His low-rank identity overrode his higher one, and therefore, the higher purpose of the role.

To follow the noble goal of the role, we need to identify with the positional power of our role. We need to use our personal power to rise to the challenge. In our high-power roles, we are serving something larger than ourselves, we owe allegiance to the role, the organization or community, and even the profession. There may be just one noble goal of your role (i.e., "First, Do No Harm"), or there may be several. For some, they are clear, and belong to the industry (medicine, psychology) or profession (teaching), for others, they may be less clear, and open to your own interpretation. For instance, for some business people I have worked with, the noble goal is to put the customer's interests first, for others it is to serve the organization, and for others still, it is to return value to the society, whether through creating jobs, protecting the environment, or philanthropy.

Doable Practice #14: Fulfill the Noble Goal of the Role

Think about the heroes and mentors in your field, those people in your profession or discipline you look up to. What qualities do they embody? What values have they stood for, championed, and promoted? Next, ask yourself, if there was one thing you would like people to say about you after your death, what do you hope they would say?

Look at these two answers. What do they have in common, and what do they tell you about your own personal noble goal of the role? How well do you feel you are doing following the noble goal? Are there ways in which you can improve?

We are now at the end of the guidelines for power. It's only a beginning: as you use your power, you will no doubt learn more. Power is an incredible teacher, and if we stay open to feedback and watch out for our own self-confirming beliefs, power will teach us what we need to know about its use.

The final chapter looks into the special challenges power can unearth. In a way, every situation is complex, but certain uses of power require more awareness and skill. What happens if we are the first among our marginalized group to occupy a position of power in the public eye? How do we manage those situations where we have less power, yet want to make an impactful change or influence bosses, superiors, or the powers that be? What about power in the helping and guiding professions—where much of our work is done in private, without direct supervision, and the relationship with our client is of an intimate nature—such as in therapy, coaching, and healing? The next chapter will show you the skills and attitudes you need to manage these special challenges.

8

Troubleshooting: Special Power Challenges

~⌒

To gain your own voice, forget about having it heard.
Become a saint of your own province and your own consciousness.
—ALLEN GINSBERG

The most common way people give up their power
is by thinking they don't have any.
—ALICE WALKER

It's hard enough to get power right under ideal circumstances. And ideal situations are the rare ones. Most of us, most of the time, are challenged to use power in tough or seemingly impossible situations: against towering opposition, lacking the support of others, attempting to change an established and entrenched authority or influence another group's agenda when we lack fellowship in that group.

The fourteen guidelines described in Chapters 5–7 are a power user's foundation, applicable to anyone and for any use of power. These extra guidelines on special challenges are meant to address circumstances that require more than the fundamentals.

Each one of these guidelines warrants its very own book. In this book, I will only describe three special challenges I see most frequently in my work with people in power, and highlight some of the more crucial attitudes, skills, and considerations to keep in mind. These challenges are:

1) ***Breaking Down Barriers:*** What happens when you are one of the first of a marginalized group to occupy a position of power? How do you navigate the outsized expectations, stereotyping, tokenism, and daily micro-aggressions you may encounter?

2) ***Leading Up:*** How do we influence those who have more rank (be they a boss, teacher, parent, or community leader) or as a means to challenge the status quo? How do we use our power effectively and in tandem with someone or a group that has power over us?

3) ***The Trusted Advisor:*** How do you stay mindful and in service to your client in a role characterized by intimacy, dependency, admiration, and expertise—a role such as a doctor, therapist, coach, clergy person, or mentor?

Challenge #1: Breaking Down Barriers

"I am not the Catholic candidate for president. I am the Democratic Party candidate for president who also happens to be a Catholic." So said John F. Kennedy Jr. in 1960. He was trying to dispel fears of a Catholic president. Many of us don't remember or didn't experience the anti-Catholic sentiment of the early 20th century, yet Kennedy had to battle prejudice and fear that someone in his position, with his religious beliefs, would take orders from the Pope, and not from his people. To this day, Kennedy remains the only non-Protestant U.S. president.

Fifty years later, Barack Obama said, "I am the president of the United States of America, not the United States of black America" to fellow black Americans who had accused him of not prioritizing the needs of African Americans during his first term in office. As the first black president of the United States, Obama shouldered an enormous burden of stereotyping, prejudice, and the unrealistic positive and negative expectations placed on him by black and white Americans alike.

Franklin Delano Roosevelt was the first and only U.S. president with a known physical disability. Although today some see him as a champion for disabled rights, during his lifetime he never permitted himself to be photographed in a wheelchair and never publicly acknowledged his polio. He hid his disability from view to alleviate any possible anxieties or prejudices people may have had about him.

We don't come into our roles of power as blank slates. We carry with us our social identities: African American, Asian, Asian American, first-generation, second-generation, female, transgendered, agendered, gay, bisexual, straight, Protestant, Catholic, Muslim, Jewish, disabled, and differently-abled. Some people's social identities encumber them with stereotypes, prejudice, and larger-than-life expectations. When you are the first of your social group to step into a powerful, public role, your fate is to carry these extra loads. Every action, every decision, every facial gesture and behavior will be scrutinized and analyzed, judged and interpreted, dismissed or discussed—all through the filter of one's social identity.

Every leader, not only those who hail from a marginalized social group, learns to habituate to public criticism, second-guessing by pundits, and condemnation from political adversaries. But if you are a member of a marginalized identity, you are the target of not just criticism, but also hatred: you are subject to a whole other, emotional, category of misery.

Julia Gillard, the first female Prime Minister of Australia, endured pornographic cartoons, slurs, and sexist jokes. These offenses sprouted not only from social and news media, but also from members of Parliament. The same is true for Obama and his family; the outpouring of racist comments, death threats, hate speech, jokes, and cartoons following his election caught many around the world by surprise.

It's beyond criticism. Death threats, misogynist and racist comments, fabricated stories about your personal life or sexuality or looks of you and your family—circulating freely in the media and on the Internet—is harassment. If any of that happened in a workplace, we would sue our employer for discrimination or for not creating a safe workplace. Public service leaders at the top, however, do not have the privilege of suing. They can't complain or attack back. They have little choice but to endure it. It's part of the exceptional fate for leaders who go "first," those uncommonly brave individuals who break through a glass ceiling.

When you are the first of your marginalized group to rise to a place of prominence, in addition to racism, sexism, and other "isms" you suffer, you have to manage a bevy of unique problems: the pressure to minimize the threat you pose, the burden of stereotypes and unrealistic expectations, the disabling effects of tokenism, and the accusation from those within your group that you've "sold out."

This could be the most challenging "special power challenge" there is. Here's why:

Difficulty #1: Minimizing the threat of difference. To allay the anxieties of the mainstream, as a member of a marginalized group you have to minimize your social identity, claiming that, like Kennedy and Obama, you just "happen to be" Catholic or black. This minimization of social identity is meant to alleviate the anxiety of a prevailing public sentiment whose prejudices and biases render people and their social identity marginal in the first place.

Minimizing difference makes people comfortable because it emphasizes a common humanity, but it comes at a cost. Our social identity shouldn't have to be minimized; we should also be able to highlight and celebrate our differences. The unique differences our social identity provides are not just sources of personal value—they're also things the mainstream needs to learn about.

Elected in 2013, Mayor Bill de Blasio of New York City is the first white politician in U.S. history to serve in public office with a black spouse. When he won the election, and took the stage with his wife, Chirlane McCray, and their two biracial children, the public saw something remarkable and rare.

Interracial marriage is still not widely accepted in the United States. To illustrate this point: in 2014, the cereal brand Cheerios ran an ad featuring an interracial family. The spot received so many racist comments the company decided to take it down, determining the ad wasn't "family friendly."[1]

DeBlasio's marriage is exceptional for another reason: within the number of interracial unions, the least common is between a white man and a black woman. While subject to prejudiced reactions, their appearance in the public eye has also been inspirational. Many have written about the positive and uplifting message their marriage sends. It's been especially significant to children of interracial marriages, who often feel isolated from multiple communities.[2]

What we're minimizing is not our social identity, but the *stereotype* it carries. That stereotype does not belong to our social identity; it belongs to the broad ignorance that created it in the first place. Breaking down barriers puts us in a painful, paradoxical position. By minimizing who we are, we can actually add fuel to the stereotype by not challenging it, but seeking to alleviate it.

Assimilation is a long tradition. Some people have endeavored to minimize what's different about them or their culture to such a degree that they appear to have disowned the differences or forgotten about them altogether. We hide our social features (if we can), change our names, act straight, white, Christian, or masculine to fit in with the mainstream image of our role. The list of major movie stars who started life with 'ethnic sounding' names could fill an entire phonebook. Assimilation can start in childhood: we don't take lunches from home to school because kids will make fun of our "funny foods." We get teased for what we wear, and quickly learn to dress like the other kids. We use nicknames that are more pronounceable. We learn quickly to distance ourselves from stereotypical behaviors that would cause people to view us as enacting a negative stereotype and as therefore unsuited for the role we have. Women in executive positions cannot be emotional, black leaders cannot express anger—it would just confirm the stereotype.

Sometimes assimilation takes the form of disowning your group. You end up hating others from your ethnic group, or wanting nothing to do with them. Loss of cultural and ethnic heritage is an unquantifiable cost of assimilation, but the loss grows even wider when it extends to internalized oppression, to self-hatred. What we subsume when we assimilate is not only mainstream culture's behaviors and trappings, but also its prejudice. As W. E. B. Du Bois wrote so many years ago: "But the facing of so vast a prejudice could not but bring the inevitable self-questioning, self-disparagement, and lowering of ideals which ever accompany repression and breed in an atmosphere of contempt and hate."[3]

Difficulty #2: Tokenism. As the first, or among the first, of your marginalized group, you're subject to the effects of tokenism. You're one of a handful, or perhaps the only person in your social category at your workplace or at your level. As a distinct and visible minority, you're tasked to live with the feeling—your feelings and others'—that you were hired to satisfy a quota, to "tick off a box," or to show compliance with the letter but not the spirit of a "diversity law." Thus, you face monumental pressure to prove you deserved the spot on the basis of your skills. You're in a seemingly inescapable bind: you're subject to higher-than-average expectations to succeed despite prejudice; and at the same time, because others believe you were brought on for reasons other than merit, you lack others' trust, and often arrive in the position debilitated by the hiring itself.

If that isn't strenuous enough, people in your midst routinely expect you represent the entire diversity of your social group. Everything you do gets seen as typical of where you come from. This compounds your loneliness. You feel isolated at the workplace because no one else shares your group affinity, and you often feel excluded by co-workers. And you're also alone because rather than being seen as an individual, you're "one of them"—a social category, but not a distinct person.

Difficulty #3: Being accused of being a "sellout." When you are among the first of your marginalized group to reach a level of success, you carry the group's hopes and expectations. This is a different burden to bear; inevitably, you'll disappoint some, because it's impossible to live up to the requirements of an entire category. The social group is far too diverse to be represented by any one person. And yet, because you're the first on the public stage, that's exactly what you're expected to do. So others will invariably accuse you of "selling out"—leaving your authentic identity behind—or insufficiently representing your people.

As president, Barack Obama has come under fire from black Americans who feel he has pandered too much to the white mainstream. When he was a candidate, some pundits claimed he wasn't "black enough."

Facebook COO, Sheryl Sandberg, wrote *Lean In: Women, Work, and the Will to Lead*, exhorting women to be more powerful in pursuit of their ambitions. Many high-profile women, while careful not to criticize Sandberg outright, immediately distanced themselves from the issue, asserting it wasn't representative of their experience. Others criticized her for speaking only to a small percentage of women (mostly white, and upper- and middle-class) in leadership roles.

In 1993, the first Hollywood movie about homosexuality with a major actor premiered. In *Philadelphia,* Tom Hanks portrayed a wealthy gay lawyer who sued his employers for discrimination when they fired him after finding out he had AIDS. Hanks won an Oscar for his performance, but many within the gay community excoriated the movie for not "really" depicting the homosexual experience: the main character was rich, had a loving family and devoted spouse, and could afford the lengthy and expensive trial against his former employer. Oh, and he won the case.

No, these instances aren't representative of the whole. But can one person, one movie, ever be? First is never enough. And why should it be? There are too many untold stories, hidden histories, and individual differences that have been in the shadows and need to be a part of everyday life. It's society's burden, and too colossal for any one person to bear.

So how do we manage public attack when it's not only personal, but also political: an attack on our social identity? There is no simple answer—it's a cultural problem that requires a cultural solution. Yet there are some things we can do, measures we can take to help us overcome these pressures.

Solution 1.1. Think long and hard about whether it's right for you.
When you are a member of a marginalized group, you become a trigger for cultural conversation. It takes an exceptional kind of personality to be a "first." Not everyone can do it, nor, perhaps, should everyone. Obliging yourself and your loved ones to live in the harsh glare of the spotlight is a decision you need to carefully consider. Talk about it with friends, family, and your closest advisors. Talk about it especially with those who will share the brunt of abuse: your partner and children. What will it do to your family? Can they bear that cost? Are they willing to?

Consider as well the impact of public abuse: it hurts feelings and bodies alike. It takes a toll on our health. The stress of abuse and oppression is real, and has very real results. No matter how high your rank, bullying, abuse, and harassment can be lethal. Oppression and discrimination are stressors, and ample evidence suggests stressors lead to poor health outcomes such as depression, anxiety, hypertension, and breast cancer, as well increased risk for high blood pressure, substance use, and obesity.[4]

Take your caution seriously. Don't let your own or others' desire for you to champion the cause overshadow these realities. Only when you have carefully and thoroughly weighed the costs of the sacrifice, and decided it's worth proceeding with, should you move ahead. Remember, it's a role. If you don't do it, someone else will. Your organization or society may need it, but do you? You don't have to give up your comfort, and potentially the health of your family and relationships, for the common good. You have a choice.

If you do decide to make the choice, you are not obligated to continue if it's not right for you. You don't have to be a hero, savior, or martyr. You're human, and you can let other humans step forward. The task of righting social wrongs cannot rest on one set of shoulders alone.

Solution 1.2. Make it part of the larger conversation. It is virtually impossible for you, the person in leadership, to discuss the "undiscussable," your minority status. And yet, on a regular basis, others will: others will constantly hurl racist, sexist, and discriminatory comments and attacks your way. It may not be a personal attack, but a larger social conversation trying—and needing—to happen, but it can still be personal to you.

Culture evolves through conflict. It's a painful reality. The slow, steady march of progress happens through clash and violence. It's not the only way cultures and individuals change, but it's one that is often all-too common.

In a high-profile role, it's hard to discuss this phenomenon, because it can compromise our authority. But if we can find a way to speak about it, and to use our personal story for collective learning, we place the focus where it needs to be: not on us personally, but on society. Allowing for that conversation to happen vaults the discussion beyond vilification and surface-level stereotypes, and onto the deeper issues that need working out. It's a feat almost impossible to accomplish, and yet it's an important opportunity to lead the conversation.

Do not attempt this lightly. As a leader, you run the risk of being accused of using your minority experience as an excuse. Others may claim you are "playing the race card" or "playing the gender card." But there are times when the conversation *is* about race or gender. And part of being a leader is stepping forward to air it out.

During the 2008 campaign, the Reverend Jeremiah Wright, Obama's former pastor, came under fire for controversial remarks he made about racism and white America. Obama initially sought to distance himself from Wright, but as the media scrutiny over Wright and his sermons heightened, Obama decided to weigh in. In his speech "A More Perfect Union," he spoke passionately, personally, and openly about being a black man in America, about having a mother from Kansas and a father from Kenya. He strove to explain racial anger to white America. Those who heard or read it widely regarded his speech as one of the most important of his candidacy. It has even been credited with winning him the election.[5]

Solution 1.3. Speak up against bullying. Julia Gillard, the first female prime minister of Australia, has said the one thing she got "absolutely wrong" about being the first female PM was making "the assumption that the maximum reaction to being [the first female] prime minister would manifest itself in the first few months of doing the job; that would be its height."[6] She believed that, with time, the gendered criticism would level out and people would come to judge her on the basis of her policies and effectiveness. Instead, what she discovered is that the attitude grew worse and worse, and became a "convenient cudgel of criticism" for people to swing whenever they disagreed with her about an issue. In retrospect, she says, she should have confronted it head-on from the outset.

We don't usually think of the abuse and criticism heaped on leaders as a form of bullying, but that's exactly what it is. The rank of the target doesn't change the nature of bullying. Bullies have to be confronted. It might not be the job we signed up for, but if we simply ignore it, or tough it out, we send the message that we co-sign, that leaders can and should just weather through and "take it."

"Taking it" is the wrong message to send about bullying. It's also the wrong message about rank. What it communicates is that it doesn't matter if people in high rank are the targets of aggression; it's okay to attack them for the rank they hold.

That's merely another form of harassment, and it overlooks the human beings who stand in that role. If people in high rank can be attacked, it follows that people in lower-ranking roles don't have to be held accountable because of their status. It's a feudal understanding of power and it patronizes people in high- and low-ranking roles equally. Think back to the earlier guidelines and you'll see how both messages are incorrect: low rank is not an excuse to abandon our personal power and enact aggression, and high rank isn't a façade behind which we can hide our human vulnerability.

Bullying has always existed, but it is heightened today by the anonymity of the Internet. Our public positions allow us to do something about it—if not for us, then for society. Racist and discriminatory remarks are forms of anonymous bullying. The target isn't one actual person, but a stereotype—an imagined person or group borne of the bully's own prejudiced mind. Naming this breed of cruelty and calling it out in public unmasks anonymity.

This doesn't mean you must complain about every abuse. It doesn't mean you have to go after all people who criticize you. Speaking about it may not be possible. Society might not be able to appreciate sensitivity in a leader. You may be called "weak," "soft," and "easily offended." You will no doubt be criticized for leaning on your identity, i.e. playing the race or gender card. But it can be done, even subtly and indirectly. Simply naming bullying raises awareness. It's your call; "toughing it out" may be necessary, but humanizing the role of leader by setting boundaries, allowing others to see the material impact of attack, and standing up for yourself and your family is a necessary step in curtailing cultural tolerance of the hostile behavior.

Solution 1.4. Don't isolate yourself. It's lonely at the top. It's especially lonely when your fate calls for breaking down barriers. You have the fate of a stranger: you don't belong to the mainstream group you're breaking into, but your unique experience of having infiltrated their ranks removes you, in part, from your original social group. You have experienced something others have not, and you may not recognize your familiar, former self. You bear yet another form of loneliness, the loneliness that comes from stepping forward. No matter their social identity, whoever steps forward first incurs respect along with resentment, gratitude along with jealousy, for daring to believe in their power.

Those who undergo this transition could have a tendency to isolate themselves. You may withdraw from public events. Your closest friends and even family may not understand what you're going through. You may feel you can't really open up about it, that no one else would understand. It's a lonely and isolating experience. You carry a great deal of pain, much of which cannot be shared. With further isolation, that pain can turn to bitterness and resentment.

Try not to withdraw. Don't isolate yourself. Seek the comfort of friends and allies. They may come from unexpected places, but there are those rare individuals who can be confidants, can understand your experience, and can be trusted. Don't deny your need for self-care: you may need friends, family, coaches, and even the help of a professional to help you manage the stress, pressure, and hostilities directed at your role.

And don't forget the one other group you already belong to: an historical one. You belong to the ages. You will take your place among those people throughout history who broke down barriers, led the way for social change, and—like you—paid the inhuman, superhuman price for it.

Challenge #2: Leading Up

"Leading Up" sounds like an oxymoron. But no matter how high your rank or important your leadership role, most people in charge have to become as adept at using power to influence people above them as they do below. Leading up isn't just an organizational necessity; it's a necessity for life. Whoever we are, whatever we do in life, we will come into contact with people with power above us. Even if we're the CEO, we have to report to a board of directors. Whenever we need to influence someone else, and our need is greater than theirs, our lower bargaining role automatically puts us into a lower-rank position even though they have no positional power over us.

And all of us must answer to our context. Presenting a petition to your city council to fix the potholes on your street, asking for an extension on an essay from your teacher, and speaking to a police officer could all be considered cases of leading up.

John J. Gabarro and John P. Kotter first introduced *leading up*, or "managing your boss," as they called it, in their article for *Harvard Business Review.*[7] The problem of leading up lies in how to adapt to and work with your boss's style, and how to assist them in managing you. In other words, it means actively being a subordinate.

Remember your Powerprint? We all have both high and low rank, and though it can seem daunting or impossible at times to think about using our power to influence those above us, we are experts at leading up. We spend our entire childhood in lower-rank, or subordinate roles: as children, students, younger siblings maybe, as minors and dependents, and often somewhere in the pecking order within our peer group. If you're reading this, you already have a tremendous number of skills in leading up, and yet you're hindered by certain parameters and constraints in your organizational context. You have to answer to others, you have to follow a protocol that limits what you can say or do, your higher-ups may dismiss your ideas or contribution out of hand, you're not privy to information needed to make informed decisions, et cetera. But there are things you can do, attitudes you can adopt, to become more successful in your low-rank role. Most importantly, to be able to contribute successfully, *don't overestimate others' positional power, be a partner,* and *remember your rank.*

Solution 2.1. Don't overestimate positional power. The most significant way we lose our power, go astray, and mismanage our relationships with those in authority is to overestimate the other person's positional power. Alice Walker's quote at the beginning of this chapter should be a mantra for any time we have to lead up: the quickest way you lose power is by thinking you don't have any. It's easy to forget the power we do have when we let social rank dazzle us. While leaders get the limelight, followers run organizations. Politicians live in the headlines, but social change is a grassroots endeavor. Almost all great social change came from leading up.

When it comes to positional power, it's always easy to fall into the old, faulty way of thinking: we want to believe people in power got there because they were in some way better, not just better at what they do, but somehow, better people. Few would blankly admit to believing it, but our actions indicate we consider leaders perfect.

"Perfect" seems like a bold sentiment, but when I hear people complain about their teachers, bosses, or parents, I often hear disappointment. The fact is that we hold people in power to an impossible standard. When they do something disappointing or plain stupid (and they invariably do), we get angry at them. It's puzzling. How angry do you get at friends when they make a mistake? At your children? Students? Employees?

One of the reasons, I believe, we get angry with leaders when they make mistakes isn't because of the mistakes, but because they failed to live up to the standard we set for them. We set it through our unconscious projections of perfection.

Recently, I was talking to my client, Larry, a Vice President of Sales who was struggling to communicate with his boss Vanetta, the CEO. No matter how hard he tried, he always felt that he and Vanetta were "out of step." According to Larry, Vanetta's abrupt style was to blame.

During an unrelated conversation we were having one day, Larry mentioned another colleague, Lorraine, whom everyone had difficulty with.

"Sure," Larry said, "Lorraine's a bit grouchy at times, but she has such good ideas. She brings a lot to the table. You just have to figure out how to approach her."

I looked at Larry, and waited for him to see what I just saw.

He didn't. So I asked him, "Why do you have patience with Lorraine, but when it comes to Vanetta, you expect so much more? Isn't it basically the same thing? They each have their idiosyncrasies, yet bring a lot to the table?" Larry looked at me and fell silent. I could tell he wanted to argue, and that his argument would be *But Vanetta is the boss.*

We don't give people in power a break the way we give a colleague or even a subordinate a break. True, a powerful role is one with responsibilities, and people should do better. We, in that role, should hold ourselves to the highest standards we have. We wouldn't expect anything less from anyone else. But no one attains a position of power, authority, or expertise because they're perfect. No one achieves a position of power when they're fully ready, either. Parents become parents before they know what they are doing. Employees get promoted into management roles absent any management experiences. Every teacher starts out inexperienced, thrust into a class, delivering a course she's never before delivered. Every doctor had a first patient. The role has rank, but the person may not yet fit that rank.

Humans are infinitely complex. We can be both good and bad, and neither, and both, all at the same time, depending on who's watching. We can excel in one area while acting monstrously in another. You could be a great boss and a horrible mother. Confusingly, we love our characters in the movies and on television to be this way, yet abhor the same dynamic in our leaders. The possibility that our leaders could still be learning seems anathema to our goals and expectations of the world. And yet, some of the greatest leaders in the world, the ones who risked life and limb to fight for justice, had messy home lives or were absent parents, impatient and grouchy bosses, and promiscuous partners.

To lead up, just remember that social power doesn't mean perfection. No matter how high up someone seems, we have to view them in their totality—good and bad: enlightened and amazing, stupid and disappointing. Try to appreciate the person in the role. Try to see them as you are: fallible, struggling, failing, doing the best they can.

I try to use this awareness when I find myself critical of leaders or those with higher rank: how do I want others to relate to *my* imperfections, when they see them?

Leaders should certainly do better, but faulting them personally for their failures or missteps overly estimates their power and, ultimately, underestimates yours. If we do diminish them, we inadvertently put ourselves down because we no longer see the importance of our role: to help them do better. If we make social rank too important, we don't see how we fulfill a needed and important part of the relationship: how we are the leader's partner.

Solution 2.2. Be a partner. The operative word is subordinate, but a better word is partner: as a subordinate, our job is to be a partner to our boss, to take responsibility for our part in making that relationship work. We can't just suffer in silence (or complain loudly) because our boss doesn't know how to manage us, talk to us, or relate to us in the way we'd like them to; or our teachers don't support us in the ways we need to learn. Sometimes, we have to take the lead. We too have to use our power, and our personal power, to make that relationship work.

We have to take the lead because the boss is dependent. The higher you ascend, the more dependent you are on others "beneath" you for getting work done. A hierarchical system is an interdependent one. The boss needs help to get things done, and your job is to figure out how to feed the boss the information they need to know.

It's an interdependent relationship between two people who rely on each other's expertise, support, and competency for a successful outcome, both personally and organizationally.

When you see yourself as a partner, you raise your self-perceived power, your rank, and see yourself as critical to a successful outcome. You may not know what to do, but simply putting yourself in that frame of mind raises your rank and self-esteem, and creates the conditions for bringing your own form of leadership into that relationship.

Solution 2.3. Remember your rank. Being able to be a partner means seeing what you have to offer. And that means believing in your rank. But if our self-perceived power is low, we will interpret the boss's behavior from our lower-rank perspective, and see the boss as unfair, or as an idiot, monster, or worse. When our perception comes from a low-rank-based perspective, we will automatically interpret the other's behavior as high-rank and act in accordance.

A colleague of mine was having a conflict at work with her boss. She felt terrible, because, she said, her boss was critical of her and thought she wasn't good at her job. When she explained the circumstances to me, I saw a completely different story. In fact, her low-rank perception overlooked the fact that she was excellent in her role; so good, in fact, that she outshone her boss. Her boss wasn't critical—he was jealous and threatened. Her low-rank perspective could only interpret his behavior in one way: she wasn't good at what she did. A low-rank perspective of ourselves misinterprets the other's behavior, but also minimizes what we bring to the table.

It's important to appreciate the privileges and powers of your own rank. What is disturbing about a boss is often your own problem with how you see your rank. You don't value enough what you have to offer or your perspective.

One of the ways to value your rank is to remember your criticisms as teachings. If we're critical of our boss, as I explained to Larry, maybe it's because we see a better way of doing things. And doesn't that mean, in a sense, we're better at being the boss than they are? In fact, we must have skills, perspectives, or knowledge that our bosses (and parents, teachers, and coaches) lack. To be able to truly partner with people above us, we have to entertain the thought that we can help others, and that we have something to teach, regardless of others' rank. Criticizing someone in power implies that you see a better way to do things.[8] So, value your rank. Don't only criticize—teach. Don't make rank a reason to indulge aggression: Ask yourself, "How would I treat a student or subordinate, if they got it wrong?" And how would you like teachers or bosses to treat you if you got it wrong?

You can only be helpful if you value your rank.

Challenge #3: The Trusted Advisor

Socrates once refused a father's request to teach his son, saying, "I cannot teach your son because he does not love me." This might sound strange to teachers today, but Socrates's statement still strikes a chord. Using your rank to facilitate another's learning and growth, whether as a teacher, coach, advisor, mentor, or therapist, often involves a kind of intimacy. Therapist and client, coach and trainee, advisor and advisee, student and teacher—all engage in a powerful partnership of personal transformation, which involves more than the simple transmission of information and skills.

Multiple levels of dependency characterize helper and advisor relationships: the client or customer discloses personal, private, and sensitive information to the advisor, whether of a personal, psychological, medical, or financial nature. This creates the first dependency: a one-way stream of confidential information flows from client to advisor.

The second dependency results from the advisor's expert knowledge, to which the client is not privy. The client has to trust and follow the advisor's knowledge without their own expertise in the subject matter to guide and help them judge right from wrong solutions. It's like bringing your car into a mechanic's shop: you cannot know whether or not the problem and its (often expensive) solution are right. The best you can do is get a second opinion, but that's often a more complex, lengthy, and expensive process.

The third and perhaps most perilous dependency is the direct intimacy between the practitioner and client. If the client comes to the advisor for help, and the advisor does indeed help the client, the client walks away with a feeling of gratitude that can develop into admiration, awe, and even love. This can be akin to what some psychologists call "transference," a projection of parental love and a seeking of approval from the helper, a stand-in for the client's original caretaker.

The context of a workplace adds a layer of difficulty. Most doctors, therapists, coaches, clergy, attorneys, consultants, and the like work in private, without direct supervision or oversight. The private setting also lacks the typical mix of rank and roles that are present in an organization. In a workplace setting, you interact daily with people below, above, and adjacent to you. But therapists', coaches', and doctors' only exposure to others in a professional setting is alone, with clients—those with lesser rank in need of their expertise or advice. This puts the ostensible helper into a lopsided position, and skews their perspective of the world and themselves. This is such a tricky area, one that requires so much self-awareness on the part of the practitioner, that it is no wonder these professions are subject to ethics codes, which are strongly enforced.

These dependencies can happen anywhere a mix of help, admiration, and dependency occur. The danger for this duo is twofold. For clients, their need for help and their sense of dependency on a person or method in which they lack expertise, mixed possibly with admiration and intimacy, can lower their ability to discern help from harm and make them vulnerable to abuse. For the advisor or helper, the admiration, dependency, and respect for their skills can be intoxicating and lead to impaired judgment. It's why the helping professions have rigorous codes of conduct and ethical guidelines, overseen by professional associations with the power to prosecute any violations to their codes of conduct.

As with all abuses of power, the egregious, obvious ones come to mind first: therapists or teachers who sleep with their clients or students, fraudulent financial advisors, doctors who misdiagnose patients in order to charge for expensive treatments, and the like. It's more common than we think, though, to fall prey to the lure of admiration, and lose sight of one's professional duties.

Many of the cases I'm aware of involve therapists, teachers, or helpers becoming over-involved, being unaware of their relationship needs, succumbing to flattery, and overestimating their patient's, client's or student's autonomy. I was once asked to consult with a pastor about the church's youth minister, whom I'll call Joshua. A recent addition to the church, Joshua had done a tremendous job engaging young people in the congregation. His Bible study classes for children attracted twice as many kids than his predecessors had. His teen youth groups were similarly popular. Teenagers who hadn't been active in years were showing up for his Wednesday afternoon groups.

But he had also stirred up complaints from some of the parishioners, who took their grievances to the pastor. One parent said

Joshua created insider and outsider groups, taking some kids on field trips, but not others. Another parent said her daughter had asked a question in class about a conflicting interpretation the previous youth director had given to a Bible story. Joshua criticized the previous director's answer. Her daughter had liked the previous director, and felt hurt when Joshua denounced his interpretation. What really upset the pastor, however, was that when he confronted Joshua about the complaints, Joshua responded in anger and claimed others were jealous of his popularity, and that they were trying to discredit him.

Joshua's tendency to play favorites created divisiveness in the congregation. Leaders, teachers, coaches, clergy, and others like Joshua use their position to gain popularity, but also enhance their control by selectively showering attention on their followers. There are many reasons people do this: sometimes it's to create friends, but other times it's a power play. Such a "divide-and-conquer" strategy allows one's power to go unchallenged, because those who are not fully on board or who challenge the teacher or leader are met with social isolation.

This special power challenge is a thorny one. The built-in conflict of interest makes it perpetually hard to trust our judgment: it feels good to have admirers, to have our opinions solicited, to be trusted and perhaps fawned over. The intimacy of the relationship can also satisfy relational needs, assuming we lack intimacy elsewhere. If we lack the means for perfect self-awareness, how do we monitor ourselves? How do we stop ourselves from taking admiration personally, and encouraging it—consciously or unconsciously? How do we separate our self-esteem needs from our duty to serve the other?

Solution 3.1. Be honest with yourself, even if you can't fully. We can never be fully honest with ourselves. We can never fully detach self-reflection from self-interest. But we can try. We can force ourselves to reflect, ask tough questions, and keep our selfishness in check. Even if we cannot be perfectly honest, it shouldn't stop us from trying. It's important to ask yourself these questions, and to do so on a regular basis:

- Do I benefit from and enjoy the positive projections, and the respect and admiration from those around me? Do I find myself thinking about it outside of work, or at times when things are difficult or not going well? Do I find myself dwelling on those feelings, missing them when I'm away from work?
- Do I encourage my clients, students, or trainees to be independent, to speak their opinions freely, even when they have dissenting ones?
- Do I have friends outside of work? More important: Do I have friends who aren't in a dependency role, as clients, patients, students, coaches, or romantic partners?
- Can I ask for help when I don't know what to do? More important: Can I recognize when I need help, when I am at the limit of my abilities? Do I have colleagues I can turn to who will speak honestly and impartially?
- Can I be vulnerable? Am I afraid that if I show weakness or uncertainty, people will question my authority?
- How do I react when someone challenges my knowledge or authority? Am I open to feedback, including critical feedback? Do I ever use, or am I tempted to use my expertise, insight, or knowledge to defend against others' criticism or retaliate against them for challenging my rank?

Ask yourself these questions, but also try this: imagine how one of your clients, patients, or students would answer these questions about you. And how would your closest colleagues answer? Discuss your insights with someone else, your own coach or supervisor, someone outside your work who can give you impartial feedback. Find out where you might be tempted, where you have a little liability, and look at the underlying need or weakness. What tempts you? Where and why? What can you do about it?

Solution 3.2. Cultivate role conflict. Again, think back to Chapter 7, when we discussed the need to live in a mix of high- and low-ranking roles. When our job is to counsel others, this becomes ever more critical. The elevated status of being an advisor can be addictive and emotionally compelling. It's imperative for you to have areas in your life where you can breathe fresh air, free of the intoxication of high rank.

Because you often pursue your work in private, almost all of your encounters fortify your high-ranking role. The level of admiration and respect, coupled with the lack of role conflict and direct supervision, makes the need for other roles, in particular lower-ranking roles in your life, that much more important.

One place to look for this is in your personal life. You need to make sure you have friends, intimate partners, and good close colleagues who can challenge you, who do not have a dependency on you, and who are free to risk being honest with you. Above all, you need some form of satisfying intimate relationships in your life, otherwise the intimacy of the advisor-advisee relationship could begin to satisfy that need, and it will be all too easy for you to lose sight of the client's well-being.

Solution 3.3. Develop your reflexive knowledge. Excellent practitioners stay abreast of current research and knowledge of their field. In an advisor role, however, it's not enough to learn more *in* your field; you have to learn more *about* your field, too, by learning things outside of it. Here's why: We attain the rank associated with our role from our expertise, often an expertise others aren't qualified to challenge. Then there's ego, with the self-serving interest to stay in the feel-good role of expert. Finally, we have to consider our tendency toward confirmation bias—the proclivity to confirm what we already know and believe to be true.

In this role, beyond any others, we need to challenge our knowledge and preferred way of thinking. We need to constantly critique our theories and methods by drawing on research and knowledge from a divergent model or paradigm. We need to foster a reflexive awareness of our work: the ability to critique our behavior in light of our motivations, biases, culture, rank, and needs. If we are dispensing advice, it's important to understand how our methods and knowledge relate to, stand within, complement or contradict other practices and modalities. If we're dispensing expertise based solely on our own knowledge base, then we are simply asking others to act on faith, to uncritically follow our methods.

One way to challenge your knowledge is through coaching and supervising, having a teacher, colleague, mentor, or supervisor to whom you can go for advice. Many therapists do this and are required to for their work. Sometimes, though, a supervisor can grow too close; they share the same method, or the two of you work closely together, and a comforting friendship develops. On one hand, this is an inevitable, and even desirable, outcome. But the downside is that your supervisor might not see you clearly. Challenging your bias means keeping an eye on your relationships with those around you and, if necessary, seeking people outside your community, specialization, method, and workplace.

Solution 3.4. Keep your eyes on the noble goal of the role. In the role of trusted advisor, keeping your focus on the noble goal of the role is more important than ever. It is no wonder that these professions, more than others, are guided by a credo such as the Hippocratic Oath. As we discussed in Chapter 7, keeping your eyes on the noble goal of the role keeps your focus on the larger purpose, and helps you discern self-interest from the other's or organization's interest. A daily gut check about our larger purpose is necessary for those practitioners in an advisor role. It's important to develop a self-reflective impulse to ask ourselves: What does the role require of me? What is in the best interest of my client? What is the higher purpose directing my actions?

These challenges are just the fundamental ones—all of which could fit into a handbook. Life throws challenges at us daily, forcing us to evolve, adapt, and grow. Power is tricky, and for good reason: it provides us with the ever-present need to understand and improve ourselves. Its ability to skew our perception, tempt our self-interest, and alter how we think and feel forces us to become vigilant and self-aware.

9

Power Checklist

*Nothing so conclusively proves a man's ability to lead others
as what he does from day to day to lead himself.*

—THOMAS WATSON

At this point in the *User's Guide*, you have acquired tools with which to scale the high altitude of rank and power. You are familiar with power's means: the psychological effects that alter our behavior and attitude. You are aware of opportunity: the perks, privileges, and social influences that amplify the means, and can lead to misuse. You are familiar with motive—your motive: those feelings, triggers, and dependencies that underlie your use of power. You now understand the importance of self-perceived power: how you feel determines how you use power.

Finally, you know the key to it all: personal power. Hopefully you have a greater appreciation for your "self-sourced" powers, those that come from within, and are transferable from context to context. You see how your positional power is strengthened and made legitimate through your personal power, and how personal power can make you effective, even when you lack positional authority. Having read through the guidelines, you have found ways to develop and deploy your personal power in your life and work.

In Chapter 1, I defined power as the ability to impact and influence our environment. Now we can fill that in with what we've learned in the chapters since. Using power well—that is, responsibly and effectively—is **the ability to impact and influence situations, across diverse and unpredictable contexts, legitimately (with the implied or explicit cooperation and agreement of others), for the greater good.**

As with all user's guides, this final part provides a checklist for you to review the different guidelines, and determine how they can help you navigate the different power challenges you might face.

Guideline	Problem Addressed	Page #
1) **Let Your Freak Flag Fly**	• Do you hide things about your style you feel aren't valuable? • Do you not feel free enough to be yourself? • Do you suffer from "imposter syndrome," afraid to be "found out"?	93
2) **Tame Your Triggers**	• Do you lose your cool? • Do you get derailed? • Do certain people or situations knock you off balance? • Do you say things you regret?	97
3) **Beware of Foreign Entanglements**	• Do you find yourself needing positive praise or feedback too much? • Do you struggle with criticism? • Do you get easily stung or knocked out by what others say or think?	101
4) **Love Your Low Rank**	• Are you afraid of being wrong, making mistakes, being uncertain in public? • Do you feel you require more authority to be taken seriously?	105

Guideline	Problem Addressed	Page #
5) **Overestimate Your Rank/ Underestimate Your Opponent's**	• Do you fall easily into power struggles? • Do you escalate conflict too easily? • Do you feel that others obstruct your input?	108
6) **Say Goodbye to "Just Me"**	• Do you feel isolated in your role? • Are you upset by people's projections onto your role? • Do you sometimes let your high rank go to your head?	116
7) **If You Use It, You Lose It**	• Do you have trouble winning buy-in from others? • Do people follow you, and respond to your ideas and directives with enthusiasm?	126
8) **Do Your Job and Know Your Limits**	• Do you suffer from burnout? Feel overextended or exhausted? • Do you ever feel jealous of others? • Do you get drawn into turf battles or feel protective of your silo?	131
9) **Get Your Needs Met—Elsewhere**	• Do you feel enmeshed with subordinates, students, clients, or customers? • Do you lean too heavily on your role to get your needs met? • Are you tempted by some of the perks or privileges your role or job gives you?	137
10) **Shake Up Your Cognitive Egg**	• Are you, or your group, team, or organization subject to "group think," cycle around the same issues again and again, or come up with the same solutions, again and again? • Do you, or does your group tend to reject or explain away negative feedback? • Do you, or does your group ever feel insular, limited, or cut off from outside influences? • Do you feel there's a lack of innovation and creativity in you or your group?	145

Guideline	Problem Addressed	Page #
11) **Don't Measure Yourself with Your Own Yardstick**	• Do you feel stagnated in your growth, or feel your group is stagnating in its growth? • Do you or your group "circle the wagons" when you receive feedback, getting defensive, or protective about your "special way" of doing things?	152
12) **Make the Rules of the Game Transparent**	• Do people around you participate actively, freely, and regularly? • Are meetings dynamic, with new and fresh perspectives being shared, by newcomers as well as veterans? • Do people know what they have to do? Are newcomers able to jump in relatively easily and quickly?	156
13) **Cultivate Role Conflict**	• Does your life feel balanced? • Do you have a range of different and satisfying roles you play in life? • Do you get fresh and new perspectives about yourself by interacting with many different kinds of people?	160
14) **Fulfill the Noble Goal of Your Role**	• Do you feel your decisions and actions are aligned by an overarching purpose or goal? • Do you ever feel your behavior or actions are just random, disconnected from anything meaningful? • Do you ever feel confused between your self-interests, and those of the organization?	163

***

During the very first session of the newly-created U.S. Congress, senators of the infant republic faced a multitude of pressing issues: How would they pay off the debt from the costly War of Independence? What should they do about the increasing tensions over the problem of slavery? What form of relationship should the States have to the Republic?

The first debate to polarize the senators concerned none of these issues, however. It was about the term of address for the president, George Washington. What should they call him? Many felt they should use formal terms of address, for instance, "Your Excellency," "Your Majesty," or "Your Honor." Others felt strongly that such titles were a nod to the British throne, and to monarchy in general. They wanted to use a more common term of address. After hours of quarrelsome debate, they decided on an egalitarian address befitting the new democracy: Mister President.

The senators' first debate reflected their and their nation's lingering fear of power—of monarchic power. The specters of King George III and the English class structures still haunted the colonies. Winning the war and ratifying the Constitution did not ensure a victory for democracy. Two hundred years later, we still struggle with problems of tyranny and power.

Democracy is still a work in progress. Though the mechanisms of self-government—laws, constitutions, representation—are hundreds of years old, the consciousness required for self-governing is still in a developmental phase. Psychologically, there is a sort of "jet lag" between the forms of government we have created, and the individual consciousness needed to populate those governments.

Democracy requires us to learn about power, how to use it with ourselves, with others, and in our groups, organizations and society. In a sense, we are still transitioning out of a feudal mindset about power to a more democratic one.

My goal in writing this book was to demonstrate that power is learnable. Though reviled for its abuses, I believe that we can educate ourselves in it to be better leaders, better teachers, better parents. We can learn to use our powers well and wisely for the benefit of others, and also for our personal growth. I hope I have managed to humanize and demystify power, to bring it down off the mountain and place it into your hands, making it manageable, doable, and practical.

Plato, no friend of democracy, said that a state will necessarily reflect the people who comprise it.[1] Power is a reflection of how we use it. Better use of power depends on learning about ourselves, on growing our self-awareness, understanding our emotionality and complexity, and exploring the frontiers of human relations. John Dewey knew this when he said, contrary to popular thought, that the work of democracy was not to achieve common good and harmony, but was the work of individual self-realization. It's not enough to elect or find good leaders; we each must find the power to lead within ourselves.

One last caveat: in using power, you won't be perfect. You will mess up—for sure. You will get disoriented, and forget what you've learned.

It's normal. Knowledge comes from experience. But mastery comes from reflecting on our experiences.

Stay mindful. Develop a proactive habit of reflecting. Ask yourself delicate and tough questions. Find a critic who loves dispensing feedback. Above all, learn how to apologize. You'll need it.

So, as a user of power, first and foremost, forgive yourself. And then, praise yourself for stepping forward and using your powerful gifts to make the world a better place.

Find Your Powerprint

Part 1: Take an Inventory of Your Powers

This section begins with a description of the five different kinds of power, followed by a chart with three columns:

Column A	Column B	Column C
Questions	Reflections	Strengths & Challenges

Instructions:

1) **Read over the questions in each row of Column A.** These questions are not just yes/no questions, but are meant to probe your experiences of power in many different domains. As you reflect on them, you may notice you have complex and complicated responses. You may have both positive and negative experiences related to each question. You also may notice that time plays into your answers: what you feel now may be different from what you felt at an earlier time in your life.

2) To help you sort through your experiences, in **Column B, write down your responses,** whatever they may be, in a word, phrase, sentence, picture, or whatever feels right to you. Or you can leave it blank.

3) Finally, in **Column C, write down what strengths and challenges you experience** relative to each category of power. Strengths may include social advantages and privileges, but they also may include emotional and social skills, or skills and abilities you've gained or grown such as self-awareness, confidence, determination, and the like.

Challenges may be a feeling of weakness, disadvantage, or lack of privilege, but could also be felt as an emotional or social difficulty such as insecurity, fear, guilt, or timidity.

Where things are challenging, you have the greatest opportunity to learn and grow. It may feel hard, but these areas are a big source of learning, and potential future strength. So, if you notice you have lots of challenges, congratulations! These will be rich sources of learning and growth for you.

Don't worry about getting it right. Just let yourself write down whatever words or phrases come to mind that describe your particular strength or challenge in that area.

Here's an example:

| **A7.** Did you have access to public education? Did people support you to go to school, college and university? Did your parents finish high school? Go to university? Were your parents able to, or available to help you with schoolwork? | – Went to college.
– Parents went to college.
– Didn't think about it much. I was just expected to go. | **What are your strengths in this area?** I feel confident and well-equipped in the world.

What are your challenges in this area? I sometimes feel I didn't take it seriously enough, and maybe even wasted my time. I feel challenged to share my privilege in this area! |

E5. Do you have meaningful friendships or contact with others? How is it for you to be in new situations, to meet new people, to adapt to unfamiliar social situations?	*– always feel shy, insecure meeting people. – didn't have a lot of friends growing up.*	**What are your strengths in this area?** *I feel strong that I know how to be alone, and like spending time with myself.* **What are your challenges in this area?** *Anxiety about being rejected; I worry that I won't ever find a 'special someone.'*

Powers

Sociopolitical Power

Power is sociopolitical. In addition to privileges granted by our immediate social group, our power operates within a national and global fabric. Society assigns power to us by virtue of our social identity—attributes like race, gender, class, religion, nationality, ethnicity, education, physical and mental ability, and gender and sexual orientation. Social status plays a major role, though not the only role, in the opportunities and outcomes we have in life: education, income, employment, health, and life expectancy. High social power brings certain privileges and advantages in the form of access to resources and information, often bestowing a heightened sense of entitlement to these privileges. There are also costs associated with privilege as well. Low sociopolitical power, on the other hand, is often accompanied by inequity, oppression, discrimination, and the others' lowered expectations and stereotyping.

Social power appears and feels universal. But social norms do change, and along with them, social status. For instance, in the last fifty years the Civil Rights era, the women's movement, the gay rights movement, and a rise in universal human rights have all significantly altered social norms and statuses. While social power does shift, from the vantage point of our relatively short life spans, it can seem permanent and institutional.

Chart A: Sociopolitical Power
Consider your social power challenges and gifts.

Sociopolitical Power		
Questions	**Reflections**	**Strengths & Challenges**
A1. Have you ever had to think about your skin color? Have you ever felt harassed, discriminated against, or afraid because of your skin color? Are you aware of any ease or advantage in life due to your skin color?		**What are your strengths in this area?** **What are your challenges in this area?**
A2. Are your family members the same race as you, or is there a mix of different races and ethnicities in your family or extended family?		**Strengths:** **Challenges:**

Questions	Reflections	Strengths & Challenges
A3. Do you feel limited, discriminated against because of your gender? Has anyone made a sexist comment, told you that you couldn't succeed, weren't good enough, or couldn't belong because of your gender?		Strengths: Challenges:
A4. Do you feel comfortable with your assigned gender? Or do you feel constrained by the categories of male or female, or limited in your expression of gender?		Strengths: Challenges:
A5. Did you grow up middle class, working class, poor, or wealthy? How many generations above you were upper class, middle class, working class, or poor?		Strengths: Challenges:
A6. When you grew up, did you have enough to eat? Did you feel afraid about money? Did you grow up without money worries?		Strengths: Challenges:

Questions	Reflections	Strengths & Challenges
A7. Did you have access to public education? Did people support you to go to school, college and university? Did your parents finish high school? Go to university? Were your parents able to, or available to help you with schoolwork?		Strengths: Challenges:
A8. How long have you lived where you do? How many generations before you lived in the region or country that you live in now? Do you speak the language of your country? Do your parents?		Strengths: Challenges:
A9. Do you feel safe, accepted and at home in the culture or society around you? Do you feel connected to your city, neighbor-hood or community, or do you feel like an outsider because of immigration status, language, or religion?		Strengths: Challenges:
A10. Do you have, or did you grow up in, an organized religion? Does it give you strength, faith, and pride, or does it feel limiting, oppressive, or difficult in some way?		Strengths: Challenges:

Questions	Reflections	Strengths & Challenges
A11. Is your religion accepted and valid? Were you persecuted because of your religion? Did you ever fear for your life to practice your religious rituals? Does your practice, clothing, or beliefs put you in jeopardy or create discrimination for you?		**Strengths:** **Challenges:**
A12. Are you employed? Could you find employment that you wanted? Is it a job you like? Is it rewarding —because of the people, the work itself, or the money? Does your job carry status in the workplace? Outside the workplace?		**Strengths:** **Challenges:**
A13. Are you physically able to participate and function in your daily life? Are you physically healthy, and do you have enough energy and coordination to participate in activities of your choosing?		**Strengths:** **Challenges:**
A14. Are there limitations, difficulties or impairments that limit your contact with others, your ability to function, or that make you dependent, cause you pain, or isolate you?		**Strengths:** **Challenges:**

Questions	Reflections	Strengths & Challenges
A15. Have you ever had to hide your choice of partner, been bullied, discriminated against, or been in physical jeopardy because of your sexual and romantic interests? Have you ever lost a job, friend, or status because of it?		**Strengths:** **Challenges:**
A16. Have you been diagnosed with a mental illness? Have you suffered discrimination, harm, isolation, or loss of a job, rights, status, or friends because of your mental illness— either the stigma of the diagnosis, or its symptoms, e.g. withdrawal, mood swings, inability to relate to others, low energy, et cetera?		**Strengths:** **Challenges:**
A17. What other unique social power or lack of power are you aware of, that influences you, that plays a role in your current use of power?		**Strengths:** **Challenges:**

Positional Power

Power is positional. Positional power is a formal role we occupy in a group or organization such as a workplace, volunteer association, club, place of worship, or political group. The position is a role that belongs to the organization. When you leave that role, or the organization, you leave the position behind as well. Some roles such as a doctor or law enforcement officer do stay with a person who once occupied them, so even when that person is off-duty, or no longer works in that capacity, they may and often will step into that role if the need arises. Most of the time, however, your positional power is something you leave at the office, school, or place of work.

Chart B: Positional Power

Think about a role or position you have—paid or not—that fulfills a function within a group or organization, whether it be a traditional bricks and mortar establishment or an online, distributed community. If you're self-employed or work alone, or even work in a small company that doesn't have an organizational chart, what position do you have relative to colleagues, or customers and clients?

*If there are several, choose **one** to focus on for the questions below, either the position you spend the most time in or the one that's most important to you.*

Positional Power

Questions	Reflections	Strengths & Challenges
B1. What status does this role give you relative to society, i.e., how is it viewed?		**What are your strengths in this area?** **What are your challenges in this area?**

Questions	Reflections	Strengths & Challenges
B2. How do you feel in that role? Does it give you satisfaction and pride? Is it rewarding?		Strengths: Challenges:
B3. Are there challenges in the role? Is it a positive stress that stretches your abilities, or does being in the role feel strenuous?		Strengths: Challenges:

Informal Power

Power is informal and contextual. People are social animals. We belong to many different groups, and though we don't occupy formalized roles with titles within them, we do play particular, informal parts in those groups.

In all the groups we belong to, whether friendship circles, families, neighborhoods, associations, departments, or in-groups in the workplace and school, there's an unspoken, informal ranking based on qualities such as popularity, seniority, alliances, the degree to which you know other members and can be considered an "insider," and expertise or skill at something the group deems valuable.

Informal power arises from our ability to align with the norms and values of the group to our advantage. Who we are, how long we've been there, how we behave, what we contribute, how we dress and talk, and how we get on with others all coalesce to make us more or less of a valued member of the group. Cliques, insider-outsider dynamics, popularity, and all those things that we refer to as "the pecking order" are part of contextual power. In friendships, for instance, some people have more status than others: they're more popular or well-liked; they're "cool," funny, or smart; they dress better or are more athletic; or they're more verbally sharp and charismatic.

In workplaces and organizations, where we have official positions with titles, we also have informal roles alongside our formal ones, and those informal roles carry some kind of authority defined by context. We might occupy a lower position in the organizational hierarchy, but if we've been there a long time, and have a high degree of organizational knowledge (we "know the ropes"), we have earned high informal power. Access to information or resources others need always carries rank. If you know the gossip, or your desk is closest to the boss's office, you may have higher informal rank because you have up-to-the-minute insights on office politics.

It's also possible to possess different informal powers within the same context. In a university, you could be popular with students because you're a great teacher. In the classroom, and around campus, you enjoy high informal power. But if you haven't published as much as your senior colleagues, you'd have less informal rank as a researcher, and feel lower rank when sitting in meetings with fellow faculty members.

You have both formal (e.g., designated care giver or child) and also informal power in your family. Intimacy and closeness, alliances, age, responsibility, biological versus non-biological relations, intelligence, and other dynamics contribute to the informal power ranking in a family. The influences of society, such as gender equality, class, education, and sexual orientation may also play a role in how informal power is distributed in families, and the informal power dynamics also shift as children grow up, leave home, siblings are born or adopted, divorce occurs, or re-marriage happens, for example.

Informal power plays a big part in determining how well we feel within our groups and organizations. In fact, informal power can trump the experiences of sociopolitical and positional power. A white man taking a course called "Women in Modern European History," in a classroom of mostly women and taught by a female professor, may experience a drop of rank during an hour-long class. Performance can plummet because of informal, contextual rank, regardless of one's high social rank. I've coached leaders who transferred to a higher position with higher pay, at a different company in the same industry, but who felt lower rank because of the culture at the new company. Their position and pay went up, but their sense of power went down, because who they were and what they brought did not match the new company's norms, interactional styles, and ethos.

Chart C: Informal Power

*Consider the different groups you belong to: friendship groups, hobby or sports groups, families, volunteer associations, neighborhood groups, spiritual or religious groups, charities or political groups, extended family, etc. Choose **one** that means the most to you, or the one in which you spend the most time.*

Informal Power

Questions	Reflections	Strengths & Challenges
C1. Do you feel valued in that group? What skills, resources, abilities, personality traits, etc. contribute to that sense of value?		**What are your strengths in this area?** **What are your challenges in this area?**

Questions	Reflections	Strengths & Challenges
C2. If you feel devalued, or not appreciated, what skills, resources, abilities, personality traits, etc. do you lack or have that contribute to that sense of being devalued?		Strengths: Challenges:

Historical Power

Power is historical. Growing up is often, but not always, a gain in rank. We're physically bigger. We're of legal age, and thus, if we're able to work, we may be able to achieve financial independence. If we're lucky, we've gone to school and earned an education. Our life experience, too, allows us to accrue knowledge, skills, and savvy.

Nonetheless, we're still subject to the lingering effects of childhood. For some people who have suffered severe social oppression or had a traumatic childhood, growing up may provide little to no gain of rank, as the experiences define lifelong characteristics, perspectives, and behaviors. Others may have grown up and out of the childhood experiences, but the formative understandings of power dynamics hover like a ghost, still haunting us and altering how we feel and behave. For Dan (see Chapter 3), who feels anxious under stress, the powerlessness attached to his childhood health problems continues to interrupt his ability to function today. Historical power can also be enabling and empowering, like Claudia's, resulting in resilience and self-confidence. And it can be a mix, as it is for Tahir: some things are disabling and traumatizing, while others—perhaps even elements of the same experiences—are empowering. Whatever our reasons, we internalize our early experiences related to power, which in turn shapes our adult use of power.

Historical power always, to some degree, informs and influences how you enact your current role. The more emotional the rank experience, the more intense its effects remain throughout life. Like contextual power, historical power can also trump other forms of social power, such as our positional, and even our sociopolitical power. Historical power is at the core of perceived power. Because *power is only powerful when we feel it,* childhood wounds can influence our perceived sense of power.

Chart D: Historical Power
Consider your historical power challenges and gifts.

Historical Power		
Questions	**Reflections**	**Strengths & Challenges**
D1. What were some of the dominant challenges you had as a child that left you feeling weak, afraid, or vulnerable? How do you still feel the effects today?		**What are your strengths in this area?** **What are your challenges in this area?**
D2. What were some of the gifts and strengths you had as a child that made you feel empowered, strong, and confident? How do you still feel them today?		**Strengths:** **Challenges:**

Questions	Reflections	Strengths & Challenges
D3. Thinking about the power you felt as a child, high and low, what has changed, and what remains the same today?		Strengths: Challenges:

Personal Power

Power is personal. Unlike social power, personal power doesn't depend on anything external or social for its value. It's subjective and intangible. While personal power can't be measured, its influence is incalculable. We describe personal power colloquially as what we use to "get by" in life: it includes our ability to make and keep friends, negotiate conflict, promote our interests to our advantage, cope with challenge, learn from difficulties, bounce back from setbacks, and be sustained by a sense of purpose and meaning in life.

Personal power is both innate and developed. It derives from traits we're born with, as well as experience—the skills and abilities we've developed over the course of a lifetime. Unlike social power, where some attributes have high or low value, personal power is non-hierarchical. Any life experience, any personality trait, can be a source of personal power; it depends on your ability to develop it and use it to your advantage. And unlike social power, the value of your personal power does not stand in contrast to another's. There is no comparison or competition between personal powers.

Each of us is unique, and so too are our personal powers. They originate and manifest in different ways. Some of us have been encouraged and loved, and our personal power comes from social support. Some of us have worked hard to surmount challenges, and in so doing have found deep, inner resources that impart confidence and equanimity. Sometimes we find personal power through religious or spiritual practice. Sometimes we're just "gritty": we have the tenacity, endurance, and perseverance to stick with challenges, work steadily towards goals, and remain optimistic.

Chart E: Personal Power
Consider your personal power challenges and gifts.

Personal Power		
Questions	**Reflections**	**Strengths & Challenges**
E1. Do you feel you have some inner resources that help you get by day to day, to succeed with friends, with loved ones, at work, and in life's daily challenges?		**What are your strengths in this area?** **What are your challenges in this area?**
E2. When the external world is chaotic, challenging, or difficult, what do you do to cope, to get through it, and to make sense of it? What are your strategies for finding a way through turmoil and recovering from its emotional toll?		**Strengths:** **Challenges:**

Questions	Reflections	Strengths & Challenges
E3. Do you believe in your perceptions and experiences, when others do not agree? How do you take feedback, negative and positive? Are you sometimes able to learn from criticism and negative feedback?		Strengths: Challenges:
E4. What do you do to manage moods and difficult states that overcome you? What strategies do you use to work yourself out of difficult moods and emotions?		Strengths: Challenges:
E5. Do you have meaningful friendships or contact with others? How is it for you to be in new situations, to meet new people, to adapt to unfamiliar social situations?		Strengths: Challenges:
E6. What gets you out of bed in the morning? What gives your life a sense of purpose: Family? Creativity or ideas? Friends? Heritage? Religion? Nature? Politics or political action? Games, sports, or fun activities?		Strengths: Challenges:

Part 2: Tell the Story of Your Powerprint

Having filled in all the charts, look over the words you wrote down in Column C and, summarizing them, <u>write them down in the chart below, following the instructions for each row</u>:

What are the main strengths you notice? Are there recurring strengths and advantages that show up, across different power categories? List in the next column all the core strengths and abilities that show up, regardless of the power categories.	
What are some of the gifts or strengths that showed up but which you seldom consider, or don't often think about much?	
What are your main challenges? Are there recurring challenges, weaknesses, or difficulties that you notice, regardless of which category?	

Using the Powerprint Chart below, list the core strengths or power you discovered, striking out any duplicates. Do the same for core challenges you discovered. Then, using the template in the row "Powerprint story," or freehand, fill in your Powerprint story below:

CORE STRENGTHS	CORE OPPORTUNITIES

POWERPRINT STORY
My most robust powers are: and come from:
Some areas where I feel less powerful, or less resourced are:
A power or privilege I have but often forget to consider, or one that others may see in me, but I take for granted is:
Areas where I might have motive, or get triggered relate to these opportunities:
Some of my most developed personal powers are:

Congratulations!

You have worked through your own power landscape. You have found your own unique Powerprint, your areas of strength and liabilities (and have also identified areas where you might have motive), and some of your personal powers (which you can use as an "antidote" to your motive). You are now thoroughly ready to enter the *User's Guide* sections on guidelines of power.

If you came here from Chapter 4, the next chapter, **"First, Cultivate Your Traits,"** will give you further instructions on developing your power. Hold onto your reflections, answers, and insights here because, as you'll see, some of the rules will be more relevant to you after having done this exercise.

Glossary

Disinihibition—Social behavior exhibited by high-power individuals, which includes acting in self-serving ways, and taking up more space and more time in conversation. Disinhibited people are more attuned to their inner states and feelings, and more inclined to follow their ideas than be influenced by others'.

Dispositional theory of power—A theory that suggests people's traits and characteristics create the tendency or likelihood to abuse power; in other words, some personalities may be simply more prone to abuse power.

Entanglement—A complicated, dependent relationship on another person; for example, relying on someone else's praise for validation.

Leading up—Using power to influence people who rank above oneself; also referred to as "managing up," or "managing your boss."

Limbic state—A reactive, instinctual mindset brought on by the sensation of threat. The limbic system is the area of the brain in charge of managing emotion and forming memory.

Marginalization—The process of minimizing or rendering invisible parts of oneself, or a group or individual outside of mainstream society.

Means—One's abilities, tools, or methods to accomplish an end; *how* an act is committed.

Motive—*Why*: the reason for committing an act.

Opportunity—*Where and when*: situational factors such as reduced oversight, access to precious resources, limited accountability, and the license to act with few checks or balances.

Personal power—One's inner, self-sourced sense of authority that remains stable and durable regardless of the outer situation.

Positional power—A formal role one occupies in a group or organization such as a workplace, volunteer association, club, place of worship, or political group.

Power—The ability to impact and influence situations across diverse and unpredictable contexts with legitimacy (implied or explicit cooperation and agreement of others) for the greater good.

Powerprint—An individual's unique map of the different kinds of power they have, where those kinds of power come from, and the influences from childhood that continue to impact their use of power today.

Psychosocial theory of power—A theory that indicates it is the *role of high power* which displays certain traits and influences the individual occupying that role.

Rank—A synonym for power suggesting fluidity and negotiability; a dynamic network of power in motion, shifting up and down a hierarchy—which in turn depends on the given context.

Role—A position, whether codified or implicit, that bestows authority and responsibility within a group. Roles can be job titles (CEO, doctor, professor), capacities in a family unit (mother, father), functions within a group (mentor, friend, confidant), and so on.

Situational theory of power—A theory that states circumstances create the condition for abuse of power.

Trigger—Stimuli, such as sights, sounds, words, or images, which remind individuals of earlier, traumatic or challenging events.

Notes

Introduction / **Power Corrupts—Absolutely, but Not Inevitably**

1) Peter Bachrach and Morton S. Baratz, "Two Faces of Power," *The American Political Science Review* 56, no. 4 (December 1962): 947–52, accessed July 2015, http://www.columbia.edu/itc/sipa/U6800/readings-sm/bachrach.pdf.

2) John R. P. French and Bertram Raven, "The Bases of Social Power," *Studies in Social Power,* ed. D. Cartwright (Ann Arbor: Institute for Social Research, 1959): 150–167.

3) Paul Watzlawick, communication theorist and psychologist, coined the expression, his axiom of communication, "one cannot *not* communicate," in *Pragmatics of Human Communication; A Study of Interactional Patterns, Pathologies, and Paradoxes* (New York: Norton, 1967), 30.

4) Arnold Mindell, *Sitting in the Fire: Large Group Transformation Using Conflict and Diversity* (Portland, OR: Lao Tse Press, 1995), 53.

Chapter 1 / **Under the Influence: What Makes Power Corrupt?**

1) See in particular the writings of Manfred Kets de Vries and Katharina Balazs, "The Shadow Side of Leadership," in *The SAGE*

Handbook of Leadership, ed. Alan Bryman, David L. Collinson, Keith Grint, Brad Jackson, and Mary Uhl-Bien (New York: Sage Publications Ltd., 2011), 380–392; See also Manfred Kets de Vries, "Narcissism and Leadership: An Object Relations Perspective," *Human Relations* 38 (June 1985): 583–601; Christian J. Resick, Daniel S. Whitman, Steven M. Weingarden, and Nathan J. Hiller, "The Bright-Side and the Dark-Side of CEO Personality: Examining Core Self-Evaluations, Narcissism, Transformational Leadership, and Strategic Influence," *Journal of Applied Psychology* 94, no. 6 (2009): 1365–1381; Betty Glad, "Why Tyrants Go Too Far: Malignant Narcissism and Absolute Power," *Political Psychology* 23, no. 1 (2002): 1–2; Nihat Aktas, Eric De Bodt, Helen Bollaert, and Richard Roll, "CEO Narcissism and the Takeover Process: From Private Initiation to Deal Completion," *AFA 2012 Chicago Meetings Paper* (2012); and Arijit Chatterjee and Donald C. Hambrick, "It's All about Me: Narcissistic Chief Executive Officers and Their Effects on Company Strategy and Performance," *Administrative Science Quarterly* 52, no. 3 (2007): 351–386.

2) Arnold Mindell's framework of rank in *Sitting in the Fire* (42) is a psycho-social concept in which power stems from the social roles and statuses one inherits and earns, and also psychological and spiritual abilities that one has developed and accrued over a lifetime.

3) Role theory is an interdisciplinary concept of the self, found in sociology, social psychology, anthropology, and some psychotherapies. While each discipline defines role differently, all views share a perspective that self, identity, and behavior are shaped, influenced, and constructed through interaction with others, and through social norms and expectations. George Herbert Mead consolidated the concept of role in *Mind, Self and Society*, published in 1934 posthumously. Mindell's process-oriented psychology also leans heavily on the concept of roles, in particular the idea that roles shift from person to person, and context to

context. People's behavior, in particular their behavior in roles of power, can be understood as the enactment of roles.

4) Mindell, *Sitting in the Fire*, 42.

5) Robert I. Sutton, "12 Things Good Bosses Believe," *Harvard Business Review,* May 28, 2010, accessed August 8, 2015, https://hbr.org/2010/05/12-things-that-good-bosses-bel.

6) Dacher Keltner, Deborah H. Gruenfeld, and Cameron Anderson, "Power, Approach, and Inhibition," *Psychological Review* 110, no. 2 (2003): 265–284.

7) G. Ward and D. Keltner, "Power and the Consumption of Resources," Unpublished Manuscript (1998).

8) Ibid.

9) Andy Hertzfeld, "Reality Distortion Field," *Folklore,* February 1981, accessed August 8, 2015, http://tinyurl.com/cl2ho.

10) Susan Page, "Prewar Predictions Coming Back to Bite," *USA Today,* April 1, 2003, accessed August 6, 2015, http://usatoday30.usatoday.com/educate/war28-article.htm.

11) Nathanael J. Fast, Deborah H. Gruenfeld, Niro Sivanthan, and Adam D. Galinsky, "Illusory Control: A Generative Force Behind Power's Far-Reaching Effects," *Psychological Science* 20, no. 4 (April 2009): 503.

12) See in particular studies of loss of control, depression and social status in Lyn Y. Abramson, Martin E. P. Seligman, and John D. Teasdale, "Learned Helplessness in Humans: Critique and Reformulation," *Abnormal Psychology* 87, no. 1 (1978): 49–74; Lauren B. Alloy, Christopher Peterson, Lyn Y. Abramson, and Martin E. P. Seligman, "Attributional Style and the Generality of Learned Helplessness," *Journal of Personality and Social Psychology* 46, no. 3 (1984): 681–687; and Richard H. Price, Jin Nam Choi, and Amiram D. Vinokur, "Links in the Chain of Adversity Following Job Loss: How Financial Strain and Loss of Personal Control Lead to Depression, Impaired Functioning and Poor Health," *Journal of Occupational Health Psychology* 7, no. 44 (2002): 302–312.

13) Daniel Kahneman, "Nobel Winner: Key Trait of Entrepreneurs Is 'Delusional Optimism,'" *Inc.,* accessed August 6, 2015, http://www.inc.com/daniel-kahneman/idea-lab-daniel-kahneman-entrepreneurs-need-to-be-optimists.html.

14) Stacy Conradt, "6 Tyrannical Bosses Far Worse Than Yours," *Mental Floss,* January 10, 2008, accessed August 6, 2015, http://mentalfloss.com/article/17791/6-tyrannical-bosses-far-worse-yours.

15) Jennifer R. Overbeck and Bernadette Park summarize how power decreases one's ability to take the other's perspective in "When Power Does Not Corrupt," *Journal of Personality and Social Psychology* 81, no. 4 (2001): 549–565. People in high-power roles are more likely to stereotype those with less power (see Susan T. Fiske, "Controlling Other People: The Impact of Power on Stereotyping," *American Psychologist* 48, no. 6 (June 1993): 621–628; and Stephanie A. Goodwin, Alexandra Gubin, Susan T. Fiske, and Vincent Y. Yzerbyt, "Power Can Bias Impression Processes: Stereotyping Subordinates by Default and by Design," *Group Processes & Intergroup Relations* 3, no. 3 (2000): 227–256), to act in ways that benefit their own group (see Serena Chen, Annette Y. Lee-Chai, and John A. Bargh, "Relationship Orientation as a Moderator of the Effects of Social Power," *Journal of Personality and Social Psychology* 80, no. 2 (2001): 173–187; Itesh Sachdev and Richard Y. Bourhis, "Social Categorization and Power Differentials in Group Relations," *European Journal of Social Psychology* 15, no. 4 (October/December 1985): 415–434; and Itesh Sachdev and Richard Y. Bourhis, "Power and Status Differentials in Minority and Majority Group Relations," *European Journal of Social Psychology* 21, no. 1 (1991): 1–24), to selectively attend to facts and information that confirm their beliefs (see John T. Copeland, "Prophecies of Power: Motivational Implications of Social Power for Behavioral Confirmation," *Journal of Personality and Social Psychology* 67, no. 2 (1994): 264–277; and David H. Ebenbach, and Dacher Keltner, "Power, Emotion, and Judgmental Accuracy in Social Conflict: Motivating the Cognitive Miser," *Basic and*

Applied Social Psychology 20, no. 1 (1998): 7–21), and finally, that they benefit from the widespread perception that they are entitled to act coercively (see Linda D. Molm, Theron M. Quist, and Phillip A. Wiseley, "Imbalanced Structures, Unfair Strategies: Power and Justice in Social Exchange," *American Sociological Review* 59, no. 1 (1994): 98–121).

16) Adam D. Galinsky, Joe C. Magee, M. Ena Inesi, and Deborah H. Gruenfeld, "Power and Perspectives Not Taken," *Psychological Science* 17, no. 12, (2006): 1068–1074. And see also, Adam D. Galinsky and Gordon B. Moskowitz, "Perspective-Taking: Decreasing Stereotype Expression, Stereotype Accessibility, and In-Group Favoritism," *Journal of Personality and Social Psychology* 78, no. 4 (April 2000): 708–724.

17) Mindell, *Sitting in the Fire*, 53.

18) Galinsky, Magee, Inesi, and Gruenfeld, "Power and Perspectives Not Taken," 1072.

19) See Robert K. Merton, "The Matthew Effect in Science, II: Cumulative Advantage and the Symbolism of Intellectual Property," *Isis* 79, no. 4 (December 1988): 606–623, and also Matthew S. Bothner, Young-Kyu Kim, and Edward Bishop Smith, "How Does Status Affect Performance? Status as an Asset vs. Status as a Liability in the PGA and NASCAR," *Organization Science* 23, (2012): 416–433; published online before print July 27, 2011.

20) Malcolm Gladwell tracked the self-amplifying nature of advantages and disadvantages in his book, *Outliers: The Story of Success* (New York: Little, Brown and Company, 2008).

21) Robert K. Merton, "The Matthew Effect in Science," *Science* 159, no. 3810 (January 1968): 56–63, and Merton, "The Matthew Effect in Science, II: Cumulative Advantage and the Symbolism of Intellectual Property," *Isis* 79, no. 4 (December 1988): 606–623.

22) Marianne Bertrand and Sendhil Mullainathan, "Are Emily and Greg More Employable Than Lakisha and Jamal? A Field Experiment on Labor Market Discrimination," *The National Bureau of Economic Research*, Working Paper No. 9873 (July 2013).

23) Corinne A. Moss-Racusin, John F. Dovidio, Victoria L. Brescoll, Mark J. Graham, and Jo Handelsman, "Science Faculty's Subtle Gender Biases Favor Male Students," *Proceedings of the National Academy of Sciences of the United States of America* 109, no. 41 (October 2012): 16474–16479.

Chapter 2 / Motive: What Makes People Corruptible?

1) See Gretchen M. Spreitzer, "Psychological Empowerment in the Workplace: Dimensions, Measurement, and Validation," *Academy of Management Journal* 38, no. 5 (1995): 1442–1465; Dacher Keltner, Deborah H. Gruenfeld, and Cameron Anderson, "Power, Approach, and Inhibition," *Psychological Review* 110, no. 2 (2003): 265–284; Adam D. Galinsky, Joe C. Magee, M. Ena Inesi, and Deborah H. Gruenfeld, "Power and Perspectives Not Taken," *Psychological Science* 17, no. 12 (2006): 1068–1074; Adam D. Galinsky, Deborah H. Gruenfeld, and Joe C. Magee, "From Power to Action," *Journal of Personality and Social Psychology* 85, no. 3 (2003): 453–466.

2) See also Paul Rozin and Edward B. Royzman, "Negativity Bias, Negativity Dominance, and Contagion," *Personality and Social Psychology Review* 5, no. 4 (2001): 296–320.

3) Roy F. Baumeister, Ellen Bratslavsky, Catrin Finkenauer, and Kathleen D. Vohs, "Bad Is Stronger Than Good," *Review of General Psychology* 5, no. 4 (2001): 323–370.

4) Ibid., 323.

5) Thanks to Jean-Luc Moreau for this example.

6) Robert Greene, *The 48 Laws of Power* (New York: Penguin, 1998), Kindle locations 202–203.

7) Nelson Mandela, *The Long Walk to Freedom: The Autobiography of Nelson Mandela* (New York: Little Brown and Company, 1994), 424.

8) See Mindell, *Sitting in the Fire.*

9) Viktor E. Frankl, *Man's Search for Meaning* (Boston: Beacon, 2006), 65.

10) Ibid., 66.

11) This concept, of coupling personal and positional power, forms the basis of the Power² Leaderlab program, which I developed together with Lesli Mones.

Chapter 3 / Powerprints: Your Unique Picture of Power

1) These narratives are drawn from the life stories of clients with whom I have worked. They are composite characters, not real individuals but a mélange of real lives and real stories.

Chapter 5 / First, Cultivate Your Traits

1) Mindell, *Sitting in the Fire*, 125.

2) Horowitz's reference comes from the movie *Fight Club* (1999), in which a group of men form a secret fighting society whose first rule is: don't talk about the fight club.

3) Ben Horowitz, "What's the Most Difficult CEO Skill? Managing Your Own Psychology," *Andreessen Horowitz* (blog), March 31, 2011, http://www.bhorowitz.com/what_s_the_most_difficult_ceo_skill_managing_your_own_psychology.

Chapter 6 / Use Your Personal Power

1) Developed in 1955 by Joseph Luft and Harrington Ingham.

2) "Dave Chappelle Maya Angelou Iconoclasts Part 2 of 4 2006 full," interview, January 31, 2014, accessed August 6, 2015, https://www.youtube.com/watch?v=o8zXTyAb6TY&feature=youtu.be.

3) 3. Evan Thomas, *A Long Time Coming: The Inspiring, Combative 2008 Campaign and the Historic Election of Barack Obama* (New York: Public Affairs, 2009), 203.

4) Dominic Barton, Andrew Grant, and Michelle Horn, "Leading in the 21ˢᵗ Century" *McKinsey Quarterly,* June 2012, accessed August 5, 2015, http://www.mckinsey.com/insights/leading_in_the_21st_century/leading_in_the_21st_century.

5) A key principle in process-oriented psychology is that social roles are not identical to the individuals within them. People play many different roles, and likewise, any given role needs to be inhabited by different people in order for its full dimensionality to be expressed. See *Sitting in the Fire, The Deep Democracy of Open Forums*, and *A Path Made by Walking* for more on roles within process-oriented psychology.

6) I am thankful to Lesli Mones for her framing of this dynamic and for our lengthy discussions that contributed to the development of this section.

7) Thanks to Karen Salter for this story and for sharing her wisdom about leadership, authority, and conflict in church settings.

8) Frances Fitzgerald, *Fire in the Lake: The Vietnamese and the Americans in Vietnam* (New York: Bay Back Books, 1972), 24.

Chapter 7 / Share Your Personal Power

1) Jonathan Haidt, "The Emotional Dog and Its Rational Tail: A Social Intuitionist Approach to Moral Judgment," *Psychological Review* 108, no. 4 (2001): 814–834.

2) Nicholas A. Christakis and James H. Fowler, "The Spread of Obesity in a Large Social Network over 32 Years," *New England Journal of Medicine* 357, no. 4 (2007): 370–379.

3) O.C. Ferrell and Larry G. Gresham, "A Contingency Framework for Understanding Ethical Decision Making in Marketing," *Journal of Marketing* 49, no. 3 (Summer 1985): 87–96.

4) Grace Kiser, "The 12 Least Ethical Companies in the World: Covalence's Ranking," *The Huffington Post*, March 30, 2010, accessed August 6, 2015, http://www.huffingtonpost.com/2010/01/28/the-

least-ethical-compani_n_440073.html?slidenumber=0ZHHXzV
%2FaPE%3D&slideshow#slide_image.

5) Barbara Strauch, "How to Train the Aging Brain," *The New York Times,* December 29, 2009, accessed August 6, 2015, http://www.nytimes.com/2010/01/03/education/edlife/03adult-t.html?_r=0.

6) Senator Kirsten Gillibrand (D) New York is a member of the Senate Armed Forces Committee, and author of The Military Justice Improvement Act designed to reform how the military handles sexual assault cases. A Department of Justice Sexual Assault Prevention and Response survey of victims of sexual assault reports that those who responded they have been victims of unwanted sexual contact, 62% say they have already been retaliated against. The Department of Defense's own statistics shows that 60% of cases have a supervisor or unit leader responsible for sexual harassment or gender discrimination. See "One Year After Earlier NDAA Reforms, Status Quo Unchanged," Senator Kirsten Gillibrand website, accessed August 5, 2015, http://www.gillibrand.senate.gov/imo/media/doc/Infographic.pdf.

7) Chris Argyris and Donald A. Schön, *Theory in Practice: Increasing Professional Effectiveness* (San Francisco: Jossey-Bass, 1974) and Chris Argyris and Donald A. Schön, *Organizational Learning: A Theory of Action Perspective* (Reading, MA: Addison Wesley, 1978), 3.

8) Harvard Business Review Staff, "You Can't Be a Wimp—Make the Tough Calls," *Harvard Business Review,* November 2013, accessed August 6, 2015, http://hbr.org/2013/11/you-cant-be-a-wimp-make-the-tough-calls/ar/1.

9) Thanks to Dr. Paul Donovan for sharing his knowledge and insights about working with "undiscussables." See Paul Donovan, "Beyond Undiscussables? Why Surfacing Undiscussables in Working Groups Is More Important Than Ever," *The Change Company*, Proceedings of the 6th International Colloquium on Business and Management (ICBM), Bangkok 2013, accessed August 6, 2015, http://www.thechangecompany.com.au/resources/articles/1611-2/.

10) Ben Lillie, "How Do We Fix Medicine? Atul Gawande at TED2012,"

TEDBlog, February 28, 2012, accessed August 6, 2015, http://blog. ted.com/atul-gawande-at-ted2012–2/comment-page-2/.

11) John T. James, "A New, Evidence-Based Estimate of Patient Harms Associated with Hospital Care," *Journal for Patient Safety* 9, no. 3 (2013): 122–128, accessed August 6, 2015, http://journals.lww.com/ journalpatientsafety/Fulltext/2013/09000/A_New,_Evidence_ based_Estimate_of_Patient_Harms.2.aspx.

12) Atul Gawande, "The Checklist," *The New Yorker,* December 10, 2007, accessed August 6, 2015, http://www.newyorker.com/magazine/ 2007/12/10/the-checklist.

13) Maggie Mahar, "Atul Gawande's Manifesto: Healthcare Reform on the Ground— Part 1," *Health Beat,* January 12, 2010, accessed August 6, 2015, http://www.healthbeatblog.com/2010/01/atul-gawandes-manifesto-healthcare-reform-on-the-ground-part-1/#sthash. K7KwHWuH.dpuf.

14) Paul Krugman, *The Return of Depression Economics and the Crisis of 2008* (New York: W.W. Norton Company Limited, 2009), 62.

15) Michael Falcone, "Mitt Romney's Middle Class Moment," *ABC News,* September 23, 2011, accessed August 6, 2015, http://abcnews. go.com/blogs/politics/2011/09/mitt-romneys-middle-class-moment/.

16) Thanks to Lesli Mones for articulating the phrase, "what the role demands of you."

Chapter 8 / Troubleshooting: Special Power Challenges

1) Gene Demby, "That Cute Cheerios Ad with the Interracial Family Is Back," *NPR,* January 30, 2014, accessed August 6, 2015, http:// www.npr.org/sections/codeswitch/2014/01/30/268930004/that-cute-cheerios-ad-with-the-interracial-family-is-back.

2) Jesse Washington, "Bill De Blasio's Interracial Marriage Shatters Traditional Ideas of Race and Politics," *The Huffington Post,*

November 16, 2013, accessed August 6, 2015, http://www. huffingtonpost.com/2013/11/16bill-de-blasio-interracial-marriage _n_4288082.html.

3) W. E. B. Du Bois, *The Souls of Black Folk: Essays and Sketches* (Chicago: A.C. McClurg & Co., 1903), 5, accessed August 5, 2015, http://www.wwnorton.com/college/history/give-me-liberty4/docs/WEBDuBois-Souls_of_Black_Folk-1903.pdf.

4) See for instance, David R. Williams, Harold W. Neighbors, and James S. Jackson, "Racial/Ethnic Discrimination and Health: Findings from Community Studies," *American Journal of Public Health* 93, no. 2 (2003): 200–208; and Vickie M. Mays, Susan D. Cochran, and Namdi W. Barnes, "Race, Race-Based Discrimination, and Health Outcomes Among African Americans," *Annual Review of Psychology* 58 (2007): 201–225.

5) Hendrik Hertzberg, "Obama Wins," *The New Yorker*, November 17, 2008, accessed August 10, 2015, http://www.newyorker.com/magazine/2008/11/17/obama-wins.

6) Claire Zillman, "Hey, Hillary. Australia's First Woman Prime Minister Has Some Advice for You," *Fortune*, June 15, 2015, accessed August 6, 2015, http://fortune.com/2015/06/15/julia-gillard-hillary-clinton-advice/.

7) John J. Gabarro and John P. Kotter, "Managing Your Boss," *Harvard Business Review* 58, no. 1 (January–February 1980).

8) Thanks to Arnold Mindell for his numerous and valuable teachings about this.

Chapter 9 / Power Checklist

1) Plato, *The Republic*, trans. Reginald E. Allen (New Haven: Yale University Press, 2006), 140–141.

Bibliography

~✿

Abramson, Lyn Y., Martin E. P. Seligman, and John D. Teasdale. "Learned Helplessness in Humans: Critique and Reformulation." *Abnormal Psychology* 87, no. 1 (1978): 49–74.

Aktas, Nihat, Eric De Bodt, Helen Bollaert, and Richard Roll. "CEO Narcissism and the Takeover Process: From Private Initiation to Deal Completion." *AFA 2012 Chicago Meetings Paper* (2012).

Alloy, Lauren B., Christopher Peterson, Lyn Y. Abramson, and Martin E. P. Seligman. "Attributional Style and the Generality of Learned Helplessness." *Journal of Personality and Social Psychology* 46, no. 3 (1984): 681–687.

Argyris, Chris, and Donald A. Schön. *Organizational Learning: A Theory of Action Perspective.* Reading, MA: Addison Wesley, 1978.

———. *Theory in Practice: Increasing Professional Effectiveness.* San Francisco: Jossey-Bass, 1974.

Bachrach, Peter, and Morton S. Baratz. "Two Faces of Power." *The American Political Science Review* 56, no. 4 (December 1962): 947–52. Accessed July 2015. http://www.columbia.edu/itc/sipa/ U6800/ readings-sm/bachrach.pdf.

Barton, Dominic, Andrew Grant, and Michelle Horn. "Leading in the 21st Century" *McKinsey Quarterly,* June 2012. Accessed August 5, 2015. http://www.mckinsey.com/insights/leading_in_the_21st_ century/leading_in_the_21st_century.

Baumeister, Roy F., Ellen Bratslavsky, Catrin Finkenauer, and Kathleen D. Vohs. "Bad Is Stronger Than Good." *Review of General Psychology* 5, no. 4 (2001): 323–370.

Being There. Directed by Hal Ashby. Los Angeles: Twentieth Century Fox Film Corporation, 1979.

Bertrand, Marianne, and Sendhil Mullainathan. "Are Emily and Greg More Employable Than Lakisha and Jamal? A Field Experiment on Labor Market Discrimination." *The National Bureau of Economic Research*, Working Paper No. 9873 (July 2013).

Bothner, Matthew S., Young-Kyu Kim, and Edward Bishop Smith. "How Does Status Affect Performance? Status as an Asset vs. Status as a Liability in the PGA and NASCAR." *Organization Science* 23, (2012): 416–433.

Chatterjee, Arijit, and Donald C. Hambrick. "It's All about Me: Narcissistic Chief Executive Officers and Their Effects on Company Strategy and Performance." *Administrative Science Quarterly* 52, no. 3 (2007): 351–386.

Chen, Serena, Annette Y. Lee-Chai, and John A. Bargh. "Relationship Orientation as a Moderator of the Effects of Social Power." *Journal of Personality and Social Psychology* 80, no. 2 (2001): 173–187.

Christakis, Nicholas A., and James H. Fowler. "The Spread of Obesity in a Large Social Network over 32 Years." *New England Journal of Medicine* 357, no. 4 (2007): 370–379.

Conradt, Stacy. "6 Tyrannical Bosses Far Worse Than Yours." *Mental Floss*, January 10, 2008. Accessed August 6, 2015. http://mentalfloss. com/article/17791/6-tyrannical-bosses-far-worse-yours.

Copeland, John. T. "Prophecies of Power: Motivational Implications of Social Power for Behavioral Confirmation." *Journal of Personality and Social Psychology* 67, no. 2 (1994): 264–277.

"Dave Chappelle Maya Angelou Iconoclasts Part 2 of 4 2006 full." Interview, January 31, 2014. Accessed August 6, 2015. https:// www.youtube.com/watch?v=08zXTyAb6TY&feature=youtu.be.

Demby, Gene. "That Cute Cheerios Ad with the Interracial Family Is Back." *NPR,* January 30, 2014. Accessed August 6, 2015. http://www.npr.org/sections/codeswitch/2014/01/30/268930004/that-cute-cheerios-ad-with-the-interracial-family-is-back.

Diamond, Julie, and Lee Spark Jones. *A Path Made By Walking: Process Work in Practice.* Portland, OR: Lao Tse Press, 2005.

Donovan, Paul. "Beyond Undiscussables? Why Surfacing Undiscussables in Working Groups Is More Important Than Ever." *The Change Company.* Proceedings of the 6th International Colloquium on Business and Management (ICBM), Bangkok 2013. Accessed August 6, 2015, http://www.thechangecompany.com.au/resources/articles/1611-2/.

Du Bois, W. E. B. *The Souls of Black Folk: Essays and Sketches.* Chicago: A.C. McClurg & Co., 1903. Accessed August 5, 2015. http://www.wwnorton.com/college/history/give-me-liberty4/docs/WEBDuBois-Souls_of_Black_Folk-1903.pdf.

Ebenbach, David H., and Dacher Keltner. "Power, Emotion, and Judgmental Accuracy in Social Conflict: Motivating the Cognitive Miser." *Basic and Applied Social Psychology* 20, no. 1 (1998): 7–21.

Falcone, Michael. "Mitt Romney's Middle Class Moment." *ABC News,* September 23, 2011. Accessed August 6, 2015. http://abcnews.go.com/blogs/politics/2011/09/mitt-romneys-middle-class-moment/.

Fast, Nathanael J., Deborah H. Gruenfeld, Niro Sivanthan, and Adam D. Galinsky. "Illusory Control: A Generative Force Behind Power's Far-Reaching Effects." *Psychological Science* 20, no. 4 (April 2009): 503.

Ferrell, O.C., and Larry G. Gresham. "A Contingency Framework for Understanding Ethical Decision Making in Marketing." *Journal of Marketing* 49, no. 3 (Summer 1985): 87–96.

Fight Club. Directed by David Fincher. Los Angeles: Twentieth Century Fox Film Corporation, 1999.

Fiske, Susan T. "Controlling Other People: The Impact of Power on Stereotyping." *American Psychologist* 48, no. 6 (June 1993): 621–628.

Fitzgerald, Frances. *Fire in the Lake: The Vietnamese and the Americans in Vietnam.* New York: Bay Back Books, 1972.

Frankl, Viktor E. *Man's Search for Meaning.* Boston: Beacon, 2006.

French, John R. P., and Bertram Raven. "The Bases of Social Power." *Studies in Social Power,* edited by D. Cartwright, 150–167. Ann Arbor: Institute for Social Research, 1959.

Gabarro, John J., and John P. Kotter. "Managing Your Boss." *Harvard Business Review* 58, no. 1 (January–February 1980).

Galinsky, Adam D., and Gordon B. Moskowitz. "Perspective-Taking: Decreasing Stereotype Expression, Stereotype Accessibility, and In-Group Favoritism." *Journal of Personality and Social Psychology* 78, no. 4 (April 2000): 708–724.

Galinsky, Adam D., Deborah H. Gruenfeld, and Joe C. Magee. "From Power to Action." *Journal of Personality and Social Psychology* 85, no. 3 (2003): 453–466.

Galinsky, Adam D., Joe C. Magee, M. Ena Inesi, and Deborah H. Gruenfeld. "Power and Perspectives Not Taken." *Psychological Science* 17, no. 12 (2006): 1068–1074.

Gawande, Atul. "The Checklist." *The New Yorker,* December 10, 2007. Accessed August 6, 2015. http://www.newyorker.com/magazine/2007/12/10/the-checklist.

Glad, Betty. "Why Tyrants Go Too Far: Malignant Narcissism and Absolute Power." *Political Psychology* 23, no. 1 (2002): 1–2.

Gladwell, Malcolm. *Outliers: The Story of Success.* New York: Little, Brown and Company, 2008.

Golding, William, and Edmund L. Epstein. *Lord of the Flies: A Novel.* New York: Perigree, 1954.

Goodwin, Stephanie A., Alexandra Gubin, Susan T. Fiske, and Vincent Y. Yzerbyt. "Power Can Bias Impression Processes: Stereotyping Subordinates by Default and by Design." *Group Processes & Intergroup Relations* 3, no. 3 (2000): 227–256.

Greene, Robert. *The 48 Laws of Power.* New York: Penguin, 1998. Kindle edition.

Haidt, Jonathan. "The Emotional Dog and Its Rational Tail: A Social Intuitionist Approach to Moral Judgment." *Psychological Review* 108, no. 4 (2001): 814–834.

Harvard Business Review Staff. "You Can't Be a Wimp—Make the Tough Calls." *Harvard Business Review*, November 2013. Accessed August 6, 2015. http://hbr.org/2013/11/you-cant-be-a-wimp-make-the-tough-calls/ar/1.

Hertzberg, Hendrik. "Obama Wins." *The New Yorker*, November 17, 2008. Accessed August 10, 2015. http://www.newyorker.com/magazine/2008/11/17/obama-wins.

Hertzfeld, Andy. "Reality Distortion Field." *Folklore*, February 1981. Accessed August 8, 2015. http://tinyurl.com/cl2ho.

Hobbes, Thomas. *Leviathan.* Oxford: Oxford University Press, 1998.

Horowitz, Ben. "What's the Most Difficult CEO Skill? Managing Your Own Psychology." *Andreessen Horowitz* (blog). March 31, 2011. http://www.bhorowitz.com/what_s_the_most_difficult_ceo_skill_managing_your_own_psychology.

James, John T. "A New, Evidence-Based Estimate of Patient Harms Associated with Hospital Care." *Journal for Patient Safety* 9, no. 3 (2013): 122–128. Accessed August 6, 2015. http://journals.lww.com/journalpatientsafety/Fulltext/2013/09000/A_New,_Evidence_based_Estimate_of_Patient_Harms.2.aspx.

Kahneman, Daniel. "Nobel Winner: Key Trait of Entrepreneurs Is 'Delusional Optimism.'" *Inc.* Accessed August 6, 2015. http://www.inc.com/daniel-kahneman/idea-lab-daniel-kahneman-entrepreneurs-need-to-be-optimists.html.

Keltner, Dacher, Deborah H. Gruenfeld, and Cameron Anderson. "Power, Approach, and Inhibition." *Psychological Review* 110, no. 2 (2003): 265–284.

Kets de Vries, Manfred. "Narcissism and Leadership: An Object Relations Perspective." *Human Relations* 38 (June 1985): 583–601.

Kets de Vries, Manfred, and Katharina Balazs. "The Shadow Side of Leadership." *The SAGE Handbook of Leadership*, edited by Alan Bryman, David L. Collinson, Keith Grint, Brad Jackson, and Mary Uhl-Bien, 380–392. New York: Sage Publications Ltd., 2011.

Kiser, Grace. "The 12 Least Ethical Companies in the World: Covalence's Ranking." *The Huffington Post*, March 30, 2010. Accessed August 6, 2015. http://www.huffingtonpost.com/2010/01/28/the-least-ethical-compani_n_440073.html?slidenumber=0ZHHXzV%2FaPE%3D&slideshow#slide_image.

Krugman, Paul. *The Return of Depression Economics and the Crisis of 2008.* New York: W.W. Norton Company Limited, 2009.

Lillie, Ben. "How Do We Fix Medicine? Atul Gawande at TED2012." *TEDBlog*, February 28, 2012. Accessed August 6, 2015. http://blog.ted.com/atul-gawande-at-ted2012-2/comment-page-2/.

Mahar, Maggie. "Atul Gawande's Manifesto: Healthcare Reform on the Ground— Part 1." *Health Beat*, January 12, 2010. Accessed August 6, 2015. http://www.healthbeatblog.com/2010/01/atul-gawandes-manifesto-healthcare-reform-on-the-ground-part-1/#sthash.K7KwHWuH.dpuf.

Mandela, Nelson. *The Long Walk to Freedom: The Autobiography of Nelson Mandela.* New York: Little Brown and Company, 1994.

Mays, Vickie M., Susan D. Cochran, and Namdi W. Barnes. "Race, Race-Based Discrimination, and Health Outcomes Among African Americans." *Annual Review of Psychology* 58 (2007): 201–225.

Mead, George Herbert. *Mind, Self and Society from the Standpoint of a Social Behaviorist*, edited by Charles W. Morris. Chicago: University of Chicago, 1934.

Merton, Robert K. "The Matthew Effect in Science." *Science* 159, no. 3810 (January 1968): 56–63.

———. "The Matthew Effect in Science, II: Cumulative Advantage and the Symbolism of Intellectual Property." *Isis* 79, no. 4 (December 1988): 606–623.

Mindell, Arnold. *The Deep Democracy of Open Forums: Practical Steps* to *Conflict Prevention and Resolution for the Family, Workplace, and World.* Charlottesville, VA: Hampton Roads, 2002.

——. *Sitting in the Fire: Large Group Transformation Using Conflict and Diversity.* Portland, OR: Lao Tse Press, 1995.

Molm, Linda D., Theron M. Quist, and Phillip A. Wiseley. "Imbalanced Structures, Unfair Strategies: Power and Justice in Social Exchange." *American Sociological Review* 59, no. 1 (1994): 98–121.

Moss-Racusin, Corinne A., John F. Dovidio, Victoria L. Brescoll, Mark J. Graham, and Jo Handelsman. "Science Faculty's Subtle Gender Biases Favor Male Students." *Proceedings of the National Academy of Sciences of the United States of America* 109, no. 41 (October 2012): 16474–16479.

"One Year After Earlier NDAA Reforms, Status Quo Unchanged." Senator Kirsten Gillibrand website. Accessed August 5, 2015. http://www.gillibrand.senate.gov/imo/media/doc/Infographic.pdf.

Overbeck, Jennifer R., and Bernadette Park. "When Power Does Not Corrupt." *Journal of Personality and Social Psychology* 81, no. 4 (2001): 549–565.

Page, Susan. "Prewar Predictions Coming Back to Bite." *USA Today*, April 1, 2003. Accessed August 6, 2015. http://usatoday30.usatoday.com/educate/war28-article.htm.

Philadelphia. Directed by Jonathan Demme. Culver City, CA: TriStar Pictures, 1993.

Plato. *The Republic.* Translated by Reginald E. Allen. New Haven: Yale University Press, 2006.

Price, Richard H., Jin Nam Choi, and Amiram D. Vinokur. "Links in the Chain of Adversity Following Job Loss: How Financial Strain and Loss of Personal Control Lead to Depression, Impaired Functioning and Poor Health." *Journal of Occupational Health Psychology* 7, no. 44 (2002): 302–312.

Resick, Christian J., Daniel S. Whitman, Steven M. Weingarden, and Nathan J. Hiller. "The Bright-Side and the Dark-Side of CEO Personality: Examining Core Self-Evaluations, Narcissism,

Transformational Leadership, and Strategic Influence." *Journal of Applied Psychology* 94, no. 6 (2009): 1365–1381.

Rozin, Paul, and Edward B. Royzman. "Negativity Bias, Negativity Dominance, and Contagion." *Personality and Social Psychology Review* 5, no. 4 (2001): 296–320.

Sachdev, Itesh, and Richard Y. Bourhis. "Power and Status Differentials in Minority and Majority Group Relations." *European Journal of Social Psychology* 21, no. 1 (1991): 1–24.

——. "Social Categorization and Power Differentials in Group Relations." *European Journal of Social Psychology* 15, no. 4 (October/December 1985): 415–434.

Sandberg, Sheryl. *Lean In: Women, Work, and the Will to Lead*. New York: Alfred A. Knopf, 2013.

Spreitzer, Gretchen M. "Psychological Empowerment in the Workplace: Dimensions, Measurement, and Validation." *Academy of Management Journal* 38, no. 5 (1995): 1442–1465.

Strauch, Barbara. "How to Train the Aging Brain." *The New York Times*, December 29, 2009. Accessed August 6, 2015. http://www.nytimes.com/2010/01/03/education/edlife/03adult-t.html?_r=0.

Sutton, Robert I. "12 Things Good Bosses Believe." *Harvard Business Review*, May 28, 2010. Accessed August 8, 2015. https://hbr.org/2010/05/12-things-that-good-bosses-bel.

Thomas, Evan. *A Long Time Coming: The Inspiring, Combative 2008 Campaign and the Historic Election of Barack Obama*. New York: Public Affairs, 2009.

Ward, G., and D. Keltner. "Power and the Consumption of Resources." Unpublished Manuscript (1998).

Washington, Jesse. "Bill De Blasio's Interracial Marriage Shatters Traditional Ideas of Race and Politics." *The Huffington Post*, November 16, 2013. Accessed August 6, 2015. http://www.huffingtonpost.com/2013/11/16/bill-de-blasio-interracial-marriage_n_4288082.html.

Watzlawick, Paul. *Pragmatics of Human Communication: A Study of Interactional Patterns, Pathologies, and Paradoxes.* New York: Norton, 1967.

Williams, David R., Harold W. Neighbors, and James S. Jackson. "Racial/Ethnic Discrimination and Health: Findings from Community Studies." *American Journal of Public Health* 93, no. 2 (2003): 200–208.

Zillman, Claire. "Hey, Hillary. Australia's First Woman Prime Minister Has Some Advice for You." *Fortune*, June 15, 2015. Accessed August 6, 2015. http://fortune.com/2015/06/15/julia-gillard-hillary-clinton-advice/.

Index

About the Author

Julie Diamond, Ph.D. is an executive coach and leadership consultant. For thirty years, she has worked around the world in the field of human and organizational change, helping individuals and organizations create cultures of learning and growth. Her clients have ranged from Fortune 500 companies to law enforcement agencies to nonprofits and NGOs.

In addition to her work as a coach and consultant, Julie is a co-founder of the Power^2 Leaderlab, a leadership program for women leaders. She is also one of the original founders of the Process Work Institute (PWI), a not-for-profit graduate school dedicated to research and training in process-oriented facilitation. She has co-authored a textbook on Process Work, *A Path Made by Walking*, as well as many articles on Process Work, learning, and change.

Julie Diamond lives in Portland, Oregon.